WORKING TOGETHER FOR CHILDREN,
YOUNG PEOPLE AND THEIR FAMILIES

SERIES EDITOR: PROFESSOR OLIVE STEVENSON

Learning Disabilities in Children

Peter Burke

and

Katy Cigno

**Blackwell
Science**

© 2000 Blackwell Science Ltd
Editorial Offices:
Osney Mead, Oxford OX2 0EL
25 John Street, London WC1N 2BL
23 Ainslie Place, Edinburgh EH3 6AJ
350 Main Street, Malden
   MA 02148 5018, USA
54 University Street, Carlton
   Victoria 3053, Australia
10, rue Casimir Delavigne
   75006 Paris, France

Other Editorial Offices:

Blackwell Wissenschafts-Verlag GmbH
Kurfürstendamm 57
10707 Berlin, Germany

Blackwell Science KK
MG Kodenmacho Building
7–10 Kodenmacho Nihombashi
Chuo-ku, Tokyo 104, Japan

The right of the Author to be identified as
the Author of this Work has been asserted
in accordance with the Copyright, Designs
and Patents Act 1988.

First published 2000

Set in 10/12 pt Sabon
by DP Photosetting, Aylesbury, Bucks
Printed and bound in Great Britain at
The Alden Press, Oxford and
Northampton

The Blackwell Science logo is a trade mark
of Blackwell Science Ltd, registered at the
United Kingdom Trade Marks Registry

DISTRIBUTORS

Marston Book Services Ltd
PO Box 269
Abingdon
Oxon OX14 4YN
(Orders: Tel: 01235 465500
           Fax: 01235 465555)

USA
Blackwell Science, Inc.
Commerce Place
350 Main Street
Malden, MA 02148 5018
(Orders: Tel: 800 759 6102
                  781 388 8250
           Fax: 781 388 8255)

Canada
Login Brothers Book Company
324 Saulteaux Crescent
Winnipeg, Manitoba R3J 3T2
(Orders: Tel: 204 837-2987
           Fax: 204 837-3116)

Australia
Blackwell Science Pty Ltd
54 University Street
Carlton, Victoria 3053
(Orders: Tel: 03 9347 0300
           Fax: 03 9347 5001)

A catalogue record for this title
is available from the British Library

ISBN 0-632-05104-3

Library of Congress
Cataloging-in-Publication Data
Burke, Peter, 1948–
   Learning disabilities in children/Peter
Burke and Katy Cigno.
      p.   cm.—(Working together for
   children, young people, and their
   families)
   Includes bibliographical references
(p.) and index.
   ISBN 0-632-05104-3 (pbk.)
   1. Learning disabled children.
2. Learning disabilities.   I. Cigno, Katy.
II. Title.   III. Series.

LC4704.B84 2000
371.9—dc21
                              99-087589

For further information on Blackwell
Science, visit our website:
www.blackwell-science.com

Learning Disabilities
in Children

Other titles in the series

Introduction to Therapeutic Play
Jo Carroll
0-632-04148-X

Family Group Conferences in Child Welfare
P. Marsh and G. Crow
0-632-04922-7

Neglected Children: issues and dilemmas
O. Stevenson
0-632-04146-3

Young Carers and their Families
S. Becker, C. Dearden and J. Aldridge
0-632-04966-9

Child Welfare in the UK
Edited by O. Stevenson
0-632-04993-6

Disabled Children: Challenging Social Exclusion
L. Middleton
0-632-05055-1

Journals available from Blackwell Science

Child and Family Social Work
Editor: Professor David Howe
ISSN 1356-7500

British Journal of Learning Disabilities
Editors: Dorothy Atkinson and Jan Walmsley
ISSN 1354-4187

For all those children with learning disabilities and their families
who helped with our research

Contents

Foreword
by Professor Olive Stevenson

One of the more heartening aspects of child welfare provision over a span of twenty or thirty years has been a growing awareness of the rights and needs of children with learning difficulties. This may seem a surprising statement, given the deficits in care which have been exposed and the obvious weaknesses in provision which Peter Burke and Katy Cigno describe. Yet, paradoxically, it is the very growth of concern about this group of vulnerable people that heightens our sensitivity and raised our expectations of professional under-standing and intervention. Thus, the book is a product of our time. It is, in the very best sense, a very moral book. The commitment of the authors to children with disabilities and their carers is powerful. They present the needs of the families holistically; balancing, with empathy, the inevitable tension between those who give care and those who receive it.

The field of disability is fraught with ideological dispute in rela-tion to 'models' of disability: that is, different ways of constraining the concept of disability. An interesting and valuable consequence of a dialogue which has at times been sharp and acrimonious is a greatly increased realisation of the ways in which society 'disables' its citizens: in shorthand 'the social model'. The history of the mistreatment of people with learning disabilities illustrates this all too painfully. The authors exemplify good practice in their sensi-tivity to social issues but they do not collude with those who present a distorted view of a 'medical model'. Acknowledgement of a child's right to a full range of support and (where appropriate) treatment from health services is a significant element in the holistic approach espoused by the authors. It is for this reason that the chapter by Peter Randall, a psychologist, in the developmental aspects of learning disability is welcome.

In consequence, this is a book which will be very useful for stu-dents and field workers who must grapple with the very real daily problems of care and management of children with learning dis-abilities – problems which often perplex their carers.

It is appropriate that the book should appear in this 'Working Together' series; Peter Burke and Katy Cigno work for improvement in what formal systems have to offer children and parents. This necessitates quite sophisticated structures and arrangements to improve communication and co-operation between parents. Chapter 10, on multi-agency practice, offers a model for this in the 'Children's Centre'.

So: this is a sound text, compassionate and realistic; a valuable contribution to a key area of practice.

Olive Stevenson
Professor Emeritus of Social Work Studies

Preface

The idea for this book resulted from an early discussion about our research: a discussion which subsequently led to the publication of our research monograph, *Support for Families* (Burke & Cigno, 1996). At the time (in the mid 1990s), we had a conflict of interests: we were keen to publish work reflecting our academic research, but we were also anxious to make the research accessible to all who participated in it, including practitioners, students, parents and their children. An academic text might not, we felt, meet all of these needs, so our strategy was to produce a research monograph, a report for the participating families, then to wait and see whether there was enough interest in the work to justify a practice text. The result, we are pleased to say, is that our initial research generated considerable interest. This text bears witness to the need to develop a more 'user friendly' book to serve those whose interests might be more professional or personal than academic.

It would a mistake, however, to assume that the 1996 book represents only the 'research', and this text the 'practice'. We found when preparing the material for the present text that we were not just writing a work about practice, as we had originally envisaged, because the continuation of our research had meant that we were introducing new material, necessitating a much broader-based conceptualisation of the practice-related elements which had resulted from our investment in enquiry. We call this our practice paradigm, introduced in Chapter 1. Our new work is, we think, also more academically relevant, because of our ongoing investigation and understanding of the needs of children with learning disabilities and the consequences that this has for their families and for the people that help them. We trust that our practice focus now complements a wider academic framework, as we have realised the necessity to inform academic parties, practitioners and consumers alike, without compromising the research or practice needs of whatever group interest is being served.

Each chapter contains case illustrations and examples which exemplify the main points made, reflecting both practice and the results of research. The examples are all accounts of real events and people (suitably disguised), not designed to fit the chapters, and although we have been careful to select cases which illustrate the points we raise, the issues and situations presented may well illustrate other points, too.

Organisation

The book is arranged as follows. Chapter 1 is about the reasons for the book, provides an initial definition of learning disability and introduces the conceptual framework on which the text is based. Key concepts, which inform practice and describe learning disability within a medical and social model of experience, are also explained.

Chapter 2 concerns children, young people with learning disabilities and their carers. It looks more closely at the meaning of the term learning disability. This leads to a discussion of how a family first reacts to the knowledge that their child is learning disabled. The concept of vulnerability is also examined in more detail. Chapter 3, written by Peter Randall, an educational psychologist, looks at child development matters and considers how parental expectations have to be linked to the progress and development of their child, whose abilities will be different from those of other children. The chapter is substantial, because we firmly believe that a knowledge of child development is essential to all involved in this area.

Chapter 4 concerns informal networks of care and the family's need for support. The concept of networks is examined together with the fact that certain families live to some degree in a state of social isolation. We explore the changing role of the family, including functional and dysfunctional elements. Chapter 5 also has family matters as its theme, but concentrates on formal systems of care and support. The concept of the family in the community, and whether support is provided by the community, are also explored. We consider the use of analytical techniques for use in assessment and discuss how these might be used to help families in need. Chapter 6 examines the experience of brothers and sisters. The intention is to illustrate the issues siblings face when a brother or sister is born with a learning disability. While we are keen to reflect the positives of such an experience, we are also careful to note difficulties and relationship problems which might arise at home and at school.

Chapter 7 is about life transitions and barriers to change. Particularly in recent years, much attention has been given to the importance of transitions in the life of children and families. These are necessarily stress-inducing, but extra support and information at such times can do much to help people plan and remove barriers to coping with change. Chapter 8 considers the vulnerability of children with learning disabilities to abuse. We look at supportive measures to prevent crisis reactions and consider how resource provision can help minimise risk. Chapter 9, on giving power to children and families, considers how individuals can be helped to become more assertive in determining their own needs rather than accept other people's prescriptions. Key areas include the growing independence of the child and young person alongside the parent's continuing need to protect.

Chapter 10, based on the research of Cigno and Gore (1999), takes the topic of multi-agency practice, organisational issues and professional values. Families can be confused over professional role and function, necessitating close liaison and communication among practitioners and between practitioners and families. An example of a multi-agency centre is used to highlight advantages and dilemmas of this approach. Chapter 11 concentrates on how practitioners can deliver therapeutic help to families. We look at the merits of different approaches and resources, giving due weight to the views of those on the receiving end as well as of groups who advocate for the rights of individuals with learning disabilities and their carers.

Chapter 12 is a postscript. We briefly give a last message to children, their carers and those who work with them, ending with the words of a mother who is reflecting on the life of her severely learning-disabled son.

Families need help to clarify for themselves the experience of having a child with learning disabilities; professionals need to inform their practice. This text follows on from our recent empirical research and literature review (Burke & Cigno, 1996; Burke, 1997a and b, 1998a, b and c; Cigno & Gore, 1998, 1999; Burke & Montgomery, 2000), where in various ways we looked at the experience of families in getting help for their child, reporting what they felt was good about, and what was missing from, their support networks.

Finally, a word on terminology. Throughout the book, we refer to a child randomly as either *she* or *he*, except where the child is (anonymously) named and the gender is clear. We use *carers* to denote all informal carers of children, including foster carers but, since most carers are, in fact, parents, we often prefer the latter term because it more accurately describes the situation of the vast majority of carers under discussion. Other terms are clarified in Chapter 2, and in the context in which they appear as deemed necessary.

Acknowledgement

We should like to thank Professor Olive Stevenson, whose support, encouragement and suggestions during the writing of this book were invaluable.

Chapter 1

Learning Disability: Theory and Practice

This book is essentially for families and professionals who are interested in increasing their knowledge of children with learning disabilities. We prefer, in general, to use the term *learning disability* or *disabilities* because this is more accurately descriptive of what we intend to convey, although we may at times, where it seems appropriate, use *learning difficulties*, especially where referring to others' perceptions or because the inclusive context warrants it. Children with *special needs* is another currently acceptable term, especially in an educational context.

People with learning disabilities are those individuals who are likely to require, through actual intellectual impairment or delay in development, some form of additional support from their families, the community and a range of health, education, welfare and other services. We avoid the more emotive 'mental handicap', which belongs to a former age and is generally considered demeaning, although still widely found in common parlance as well as occasionally cropping up in academic literature. Language evolves, however, and what might sound like the best term today might tomorrow be deemed inappropriate. We shall return to this subject in Chapters 2 and 3.

The new professional needs guidance through the experience that a family faces when a son or daughter is diagnosed as having a learning disability, the reactions that they encounter and their daily task of caring. Each parent's experience is different, and this is evident in the contrasting views expressed by two mothers:

'I saw her webbed fingers (at birth) and I thought, what's happening? I was given leaflets, but it was too soon. We wanted advice, rather than information'

(mother of seven-year-old Anne).

'The realisation of learning disabilities should not just dawn on you –
someone must have known, or at least suspected, and that information
should not be withheld from you. Information can confirm your view: we
felt we were on the edge of society and not in the mainstream. We
experienced increasing isolation'

(mother of nine-year-old Susan).

It is apparent that Anne's mother suspected problems from birth,
while Susan's mother did not know that her daughter had difficulties
until much later on. In uncovering these experiences, we will often
reflect on what might be considered self-evident truths for the
families concerned, but which, nevertheless, may remain relatively
unknown for the worker new to this area of practice. It is also our
intention that the book should offer some reassurances to carers,
given the conflicts of emotion which often leave them feeling different
and alone, as Susan's mother would testify, or overwhelmed, as
Tom's mother (see p. 6) felt shortly after his birth. Our analysis of the
difficulties of bringing up a child with learning difficulties makes use
of actual case material from our research, our experience and our
work, anonymised to protect the identity of individuals concerned.
Needs raised by the families themselves lead to the formulation of
concepts, which we think are necessary to guide practice.

Conceptual framework

Our understanding of learning disability is informed by other people's experience, but this experience does not itself provide the
necessary theoretical perspective to guide practitioners, who need
concepts as well as tools to inform their practice. Our conceptual
framework utilises empirical data, which together with a growing
moral awareness of human rights, attempts to link needs to service
provision. Individual rights, increasingly reflected in legislation,
should incorporate needs, as told to us by the families themselves.

Field research, including our own, helps us understand that
children with learning disabilities have special needs in addition to
those in common with other children, a fact given recognition in the
Children Act 1989, where children with disabilities are included in
the legal definition of children 'in need' (section 17 (10) (c)). 'Need'
means that services or other kinds of support are necessary for
children with disabilities and that these are different, by legal
identification, from the help non-disabled, or 'not in need', children
might expect. This recognition of need might also be considered a

form of selective discrimination where the use of the label 'disability' is sufficient to establish that a need exists, therefore conferring disadvantage as well as advantage. The legal qualification of need has thus resulted in a rise of selective criteria for the entitlement to services for those individuals who can be shown to conform to the label 'disabled'. Similarly, various Education Acts since 1981 have identified children with disabilities as 'special needs' children, who have the right to an assessment in order to help education authorities and schools meet their needs with appropriate provision and support. The resulting 'statement' is therefore meant to help but, as we shall see later in case examples, some parents find it misrepresents their child's needs as they see them and is therefore unhelpful, if not stigmatising.

While we believe that children with learning disabilities have individual needs, because their life course is different from that of the majority, we are concerned that these needs should initially be identified by those on the receiving end of support services. If it is not possible to identify a child's view of their needs, then their nearest family member, usually a parent (often their mother), is able to express the particular needs of their child. It is our view that professional staff should initially identify what family members say they need to help themselves and to gather these reflections on what is useful, along with professional views, observation and consideration of such needs; and from these findings formulate what should be the professional response.

In this context we shall refer to the medical and social model of disability. Our concern is not to portray children with learning disabilities as dependent on medical descriptions of their condition for their identity, but as children first who have needs which are in many ways common to all children, in certain ways similar to children with other disabilities, and in some ways unique. This empirical framework is assisted in its implementation by incorporating models for practice. In the case studies presented, we reflect on both individual experiences and those shared by other children.

The concepts we will repeatedly use in discussing the needs of children with learning disabilities are (1) power and powerlessness and (2) social inclusion and exclusion (see Fig. 1.1). We consider that in responding to these needs, the social worker requires knowledge of measures of support; understanding of how to prevent abuse and deterioration in circumstances; skills in the use of advocacy or in the facilitation of self-advocacy; and a commitment to the empowerment of the child and family. These concepts provide a

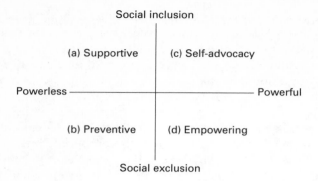

Fig. 1.1 A practice paradigm. Social work role: (a) supportive, (b) preventive, (c) enabling self-advocacy, (d) empowering.

social perspective from which it is intended to aid understanding of family functioning through an examination of the stresses and difficulties faced by all parties involved, but starting with the child.

The analytical framework in Fig. 1.1 represents our practice paradigm. It shows two major axes: powerlessness and power at extreme positions along one axis, with social inclusion and social exclusion on the other. The lack of power and social exclusion experienced by the learning-disabled child requires a preventive and protective mode of intervention at one extreme, while at the other, social inclusion and power are represented by self-advocacy. Similarly, families living in a neighbourhood responsive to the needs of children who are learning disabled will experience a sense of social inclusion, but they will also often require support from professionals who have specialist knowledge of the particular difficulties their children might face. Families who generally cope well may still need to gain a sense of empowerment before overcoming the experience of familial isolation. Figure 1.1 represents a dynamic interpretation of our *'formal and social network typology'*, used to explore issues of social integration in our earlier research (Burke & Cigno, 1996, p. 117) and developed by Burke, 1998a.

We clarify our use of these terms in Fig. 1.1 in more detail within the relevant chapters, but include an introductory comment here.

Powerlessness

Some children whose intellectual abilities are not equal to others might, depending on the severity of impairment, be able to lead a 'quality life' only if offered some form of protection and support. This need for protection gives rise to the concept of individual vulnerability. Children with disabilities are 'children in need' and so require support, but also need protection from abuse (Children Act 1989, section 48), as do all children.

Social exclusion

Exclusion for those with learning disabilities is something experienced and is not usually a choice. In social relationships, this can equate with being disregarded, treated with indifference or in other ways not included in activities. Social exclusion exists where the individual does not have a choice, is not listened to or understood; when in fact there is no expectation that the person concerned is able or wishes to be involved or has the capacity to make a difference. Social *inclusion* is the opposite of this: it occurs when the person has a full sense of involvement in the social world, and it conveys the idea of citizenship.

Prevention

The term prevention is used in both health and social work circles to indicate that it is better to avoid undesirable situations or events by offering services to mitigate such circumstances or prevent them altogether. It requires active measures. In preventing social exclusion, it is necessary to offer people an acceptable choice of support services to alleviate isolation. The concept of support is often substituted for that of prevention in social care (as is evident from a reading of many government policy documents issued during the last few years), geared towards long- rather than short-term solutions, although as Fig. 1.1 shows, prevention and support are not necessarily identical.

Advocacy

The need for advocacy arises when it is necessary to represent one's own position or when a trusted other does so for us. Self-advocacy is having the means and ability to represent oneself. Successful advocacy results in gaining the resources or services requested. However, to achieve the self-confidence to become an advocate, a disabled person needs to be given the power and means to do so.

Empowerment

The concept of empowerment helps to understand the process of moving from a dependent position (as experienced by a child) to one of independence (the autonomous adult). Ideally, the child passes gradually through phases of interdependence or shared responsibility to find eventual acceptance as an independent adult. Parents of very dependent children with learning disabilities may find it difficult to recognise such phases, or the right of their child to eventual independent living. A young adult may move to a special residential facility such as a hostel in the first instance, leading in steps through supported living to a partly or fully independent life. However, rather than use the somewhat sterile, abstract word *empowerment*, we prefer, as in Chapter 9, to talk of *giving power* to people.

Theory for practice

The theoretical framework adopted indicates that the need for practical intervention is best understood if powerlessness and vulnerability are considered as factors giving rise to the social exclusion experienced by children with learning disabilities. This may be due to a lack of involvement in family or community events, inappropriate placement in a special school or the result of institutional oppression, intentional or deliberate, whereby the needs and rights of the disabled child are denied. Indeed, parental experiences might reinforce feelings of exclusion from support, as one parent said (of her contact with social services):

> 'I saw a social worker because of Tom's behaviour and got good advice. I was told, "be firm". It worked within a week! But I'm afraid to contact them [again] because I'm terrified they will take him away. He's very active and had a black eye once. I'd be terrified of what they'd say'

> (mother of five-year-old Tom).

Clearly, Tom's mother's situation represents the interpretation, shared by many, of the social worker's role and responsibility. It could result in the family's distancing itself from sources of help. Her view is ambivalent, allowing some scope for improved professional relationships, since she acknowledges the benefit of sound, professional advice. Professional intervention, which follows a preventive and supportive mode of practice, should, in such circumstances, aim towards the protection of the child from harm as well as their inclusion in activities enjoyed by children at large. An 'included' child would, as far as possible, also be involved in professional decision-making processes. Such an approach involves listening to the child, encouraging self-determination in a variety of situations, and otherwise achieving full representation for the child. This social perspective is intended to assist family functioning through examination of the stresses and difficulties faced by all family members, with the child placed first, thus finding the best way forward to recognise the rights of disabled children as well as those of the whole family.

When considering the social model of disabilities (see, for example, Swain *et al.*, 1993), it is of course necessary to be aware of environmental factors which have the effect of excluding individuals with physical disabilities from activities that able-bodied individuals have little difficulty in accessing: climbing steps, for instance. So prevention of exclusion here would require environmental barriers to be removed.

To consider the social model of disability entails a discussion of the medical model with which it is often contrasted. Differing professional competences and interests, examined in more detail in multi-agency practice in Chapter 10, impinge on family life, usually from the moment childhood disability is suspected but certainly from the point of diagnosis.

The medical and social model

A medical model implies pathology in the individual and thus treatment is usually focused on aspects and parts of that individual. However, such a model recognises that cure is not always possible (indeed, in the area of intellectual disability and certain physical conditions, this is usually the case) and medical effort is or should be also directed to minimising the impairment and pain occasioned by the disability. This is particularly evident in physical conditions, where technology plays a significant part in treatment and measures to increase independence.

A social model implies that the problem is located in the environment and the wider context. The individual should not suffer social exclusion because of his or her condition. The question is asked, what external factors are needed to change in order to improve this person's situation? For example, the need for attendance at a special school is questioned if there is a more inclusive alternative in the locality. Consequently, mainstream education might be preferable for many or most children with disabilities but is only viable if accompanied by encouragement for the child, participative policies and classroom support. Rather than withdrawing the child from the everyday experiences of others, integrated education means that he or she is part of them.

Where the doctor cannot cure, surgery can at times compensate for some elements of the disability, by, for example, operations to improve posture and mobility, although the 'need' for major surgery may provoke controversial reactions (see Oliver, 1998). One view expressed by some people with physical disabilities is that a disabled person should not try to enter the 'normal' world as a consequence of such 'medical progress'. Briefly, then, the medical model on the whole emphasises the person's condition, illness or disability rather than the person themselves.

The social model of disability, on the other hand, is overtly holistic, placing the child in his or her context and focusing on others' duty to effect change in their own behaviour and in their surroundings. It assumes that people are not only disabled by their condition, but by the social aspects of their experiences which raise feelings of disability as, for example, in the case of a visually impaired person unable to understand the written words on a page, or a wheelchair-bound person unable to enter a building. The medical model might be appropriate in that some visual and mobility conditions can be treated by surgery or medication, but where this is not the case other remedial support, such as splint augmentation or structural change, may be required. This locates need not within the individual but in their interactions with the environment, emphasising the need for careful assessment of personal circumstances in individual cases and wider structural changes which will benefit all people with difficulties in accessing resources taken for granted by the majority.

Burke (1993) reconstructs the social model to form a person-centred assessment of need in order to show that, when needs are not met, an appropriate worker is required to assist the user in planning to overcome any barriers or difficulties in gaining access to the necessary resources. The worker then monitors and reviews the plan with the person concerned, changing the assessment as required. This takes into account the needs of the individual rather than the nature of the condition, and so moves beyond pathology into the arena of social functioning. Where children with disabilities are concerned, as with any other child, carers are also included in the assessment.

Sutton & Herbert's (1992) ASPIRE model (see Sutton, 1994, p. 26; and Chapter 11 of this book) is useful here as a framework. Its stages of Assessment, Planning, Intervention, Review and Evaluation guide the process of professional involvement in assisting with and helping to resolve personal, familial and social problems.

The medical and social models are not intended to represent a right or wrong way of looking at the world: both are limited, both have their place. A health practitioner needs to know about diagnosis and treatment and hence focus on the pathological; the social worker needs to understand, and have the skills to deal with, individual and family difficulties or problems and so is less concerned with the medical condition, except in its impact on a person's ability to deal with the difficulty or problem. Social workers, too, through their training, possess networking and negotiating skills, which are discussed in Chapter 5. Practitioners can learn from each other's perspectives. The medical practitioner needs to see individual needs beyond the physical; the social worker needs to take account of the meaning and effects of a debilitating condition.

In Fig. 1.2, we use an integrated model to show that the medical and social approaches do not exist in isolation, but in reality overlap. Diagnosis is crucial from a parent's point of view. In many

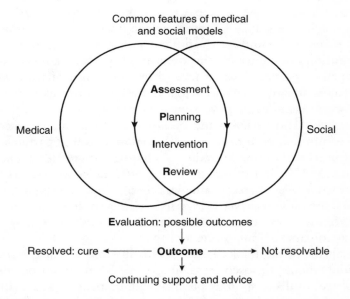

Fig. 1.2 Medical and social models of exchange. ASPIRE: Sutton & Herbert (1992), possible outcomes based on Burke (1998b).

ways, parents feel that they cannot move forward unless a diagnosis is forthcoming, often placing doctors in a difficult situation where the case is uncertain (Burke & Cigno, 1995). But because learning disability is not curable in the traditional sense, it should not entail denial of the rights to citizenship and should thus avoid an association with judgements about intellectual equality and standards of physical acceptability. A social perspective complements what should be the best medical service designed to help the child. Working together in this way encourages a multi-agency perspective, discussed in Chapter 10, where the focus is clearly on the needs of the child and not professional boundaries.

Similarities between the two models exist when the process of assessment is followed by the identification of a possible solution in either or both systems. Solving social problems is somewhat akin to finding a successful treatment for an illness, although the search for environmental and personal solutions may well be a long-term enterprise for children with disabilities and their families.

Conclusion

Professional workers need to be guided towards the issues that children and young people face in their day-to-day existence. There is still much to be done in clarifying the issues for practitioners, children and their families. The difficulty of identifying problems is not new, but in establishing links between learning disabilities and the expression of need, often limited by the silence of vulnerable children, we identify a role for support and preventive work within the process of empowering children and carers towards more choice in their lives. This develops and expands our research and practice interests, utilising both medical and social models (but particularly the latter) to aid our understanding. A chapter on child development (Chapter 3) is included because this is often lacking in the social worker's knowledge base. Knowledge of child development is essential for those involved with children and families, since it is a basis from which to begin to understand many forms of disability and identify appropriate forms of help.

The theme of the book reflects above all what we have learned from the families themselves, although we also draw on our own experiences of disability, our practice and discussions with professionals of different disciplines. One parent spoke for many others when she expressed the difficulties her family faced:

'It's a shame there isn't a person who can come round and discuss everything with you. You find out things by chance'

(mother of five-year-old Joe).

Our aim is to make such a view redundant for those who trouble to read this text.

Chapter 2

Children, Young People with Learning Disabilities and their Carers

The nature and meaning of certain forms of learning disabilities need to be differentiated from those pertaining to physical disabilities, although research offers numerous examples of children with both learning and physical disabilities (see, for example, Burke & Cigno, 1996). Indeed, learning disability is often, especially in the early stages of development, less clearly identified than physical disability. We were informed by Joe's parents of their initial concerns about his development:

> Something was wrong, because he'd ignore you if you went into the room. We thought he might be deaf, but he tested OK at one year. It eventually got sorted out, the verdict – 'autistic tendencies' ... nothing more precise'

> (father of five-year-old Joe).

Parents and family members find themselves in a new learning experience where they will encounter stress, indifference or pity, but the ebb and flow of experience, hope and encouragement will also be part of their lives, as they adjust and accommodate to the needs of their child. The relationship of carers and other members of the family to the learning-disabled child – and vice versa – is critical.

The impact of disability on the family is well documented, as the references throughout this book testify (see, in particular, below and Chapters 3, 4, and 5). Similarities of response exist for all kinds of disability, and some children are not easily categorised as either physically disabled or as having a learning disability, but may have multiple or profound disabilities.

The difficulties and concerns which relate to the task of being a carer vary across the lifespan. For many, the term 'learning disability' or its earlier form, 'mental handicap' (still in widespread use by the lay public), is the introduction to the complexities of a condition, involvement and a relationship which may well continue for a lifetime. A grasp of what the term means requires considerable time and effort. What can be achieved? What exactly is it? How will it affect us? These are questions which parents usually ask before the task of being a carer is understood, and is yet to be experienced.

Learning disabilities

The first concept to consider concerns learning disability itself. As we have said, the label helps identify individuals 'in need', because children with disabilities are identified as such in the Children Act 1989 (section 17). Learning disability in a child, once confirmed as such, qualifies the child and family for professional help and advice. Having a 'disability' conveys the legal right to professional help and services (Department of Health and Social Security, 1971). Part of these rights is the child's right to have their 'ascertainable wishes and feelings' taken into account when meeting 'need', as outlined in the first section of the Children Act 1989.

The sequence of discussion in this chapter explores the meaning of learning disability and examines the idea of an individual's vulnerability. Vulnerability here encompasses the legal view that disability confers need, hence the duty for social workers and other practitioners to become involved. The issue is what degree of vulnerability reaches the threshold for intervention, and what should be done to minimise risks faced by the child? These are difficult matters to reconcile. All parties concerned should be aware that allowing children to take a certain amount of risk, like crossing the road, is a recognition of the rights of human beings to fulfil their potential. Denial of all risk-taking greatly reduces steps towards independence and decreases quality of life (Jackson & Jackson, 1999), as some of our case material illustrates (see Chapter 8 for further discussion of protection and risk).

Learning disability: use and meaning

The term 'learning disability' is favoured by government policy (Department of Health, 1991) and is widely used in local authority procedural documentation. The expression 'learning disabilities', as used in its plural form, reflects policy development and replaces the previous legal term 'mental handicap'. The change follows reports which have had a reinforcing impact over the years on both nursing and social work practice; thus learning disability nursing developed from recommendations in the Briggs Report (Department of Health and Social Security, 1972) and, in social work, community learning disability teams were instituted as a result of recommendations from the National Development Team (NDT) (Department of Health and Social Security, 1980). The NDT promoted the policy of care in the community for disabled people, a policy which was further elaborated by Griffiths (1988), resulting in the National Health Service and Community Care Act 1990.

Learning disability implies actual intellectual impairment, and thus more clearly defines our subject group than the all-inclusive term 'learning difficulties', which every person has in relation to some aspect of daily life. We are aware, though, that many adults prefer this latter term because of its very inclusiveness, and this must be respected. The common and deliberately vague diagnosis of 'developmental delay' does not mean that all developmental stages will eventually be achieved; rather, it reflects the expectation that the child will remain intellectually less able than his or her peers of average ability.

We found that parents still used the term 'mental handicap' because for them it was more familiar as well as a more accurate reflection of their child's condition. Others use the term 'disabled' to mean learning disability; as one parent said:

> 'Catherine was brain damaged at three months after she had whooping cough. Now we have a disabled child and have to struggle, ask, fight to get information'
>
> (parent of eight-year-old girl).

However, McCormack (1992) showed that adults with learning disabilities often found the term 'mental handicap' so offensive that they regarded it as a term of abuse. McCormack also showed that 'learning difficulties' was sometimes thought to be meaningless, for one parent equated it with dyslexia, others with remedial levels of education, such that the problems for learning-disabled children were trivialised by a term that is too all-embracing and therefore unhelpful. An example of confusion in its use is found in university circles, where procedural documents make reference to 'students with learning difficulties'. Careful reading usually reveals that students with some degree of dyslexia are intended.

Disability itself is described by Oliver (1990) as a disadvantage or restriction of activity which excludes disabled people from the mainstream of social activity. The concept of exclusion as a feature of disability is important because it underlines the limited opportunities experienced by disabled people. Similarly, 'learning disability' may indicate the missed opportunity to partake in normal daily activities; for the child, the consequences can be serious. Special schooling may mean an absence of everyday events taken for granted by 'able' children, a point to which we shall return when discussing the concept of vulnerability. This does not mean that the idea of special education should be dismissed altogether. Perceived advantages of special education are discussed by Burke & Cigno (1996) and are reconsidered in Chapter 3.

An alternative term, used in the USA, is 'mental retardation'. Again, we find this unacceptable, as in the UK it both belongs to another, less sensitive age, and like other terms, devalues the individual. Until recent times the label of 'mental retardation' allowed the state the right to require compulsory sterilisation of women so identified to prevent their having the opportunity to bear children. This was based on a belief that such children would somehow lessen the stock of society, and with it came the assumption that the 'retarded' child had little to contribute to that society. Acceptance of such prejudiced views, disguised in the past as a scientific area of study – eugenics (Williams, 1996) – endangers individuals and, in the process, denies humanitarian values which should accept all children equally whatever their differences. Citizenship arguments (Dean, 1994) affirm for all the right as well as the desirability of participating in the activities which make up a political, community and social life. These in turn bring policies promoting equal opportunities (for example, the Disabled Persons (Services, Consultation and Representation) Act 1986; Disability Discrimination Act 1993).

Special needs

'Special needs' is a term used by educationalists in the UK. It originates in the Education Act 1981, which has been superseded by the Education Act 1993 and the Code of Practice. The 1996 Education Act defines the local education authority's (LEA) responsibility for statutory assessment. Special needs is a term which challenges the stigmatising effect of 'mental retardation' and promotes the view that all children with a learning disability are deserving of personal attention to enable them to attain their fullest potential. Children with learning disabilities are therefore considered special, and while all children are special, in the context of education the requirements of each child with special needs must be identified in a 'statement' (Burke, 2000). The LEA issues a statement (see Friel, 1995) identifying the nature of these special needs. The result is either selective education in a special school or in a mainstream school, with the provision of additional help in the classroom. The intention is to ensure that the child is offered the best opportunity for making the most of his or her abilities in the education system. Parental comment on the statement, which is reviewed annually, is invited. However, the following common view was expressed in these words by one parent of a seven-year-old boy:

> 'No one explained what the statement was for, all I remember is that someone called and said they would try and get Luke into a special school.'

A final point to make regarding the use of language is that, although we must learn to use the best term acceptable to the person concerned (as with any other labelling), each term has the tendency to become in its turn devalued and stigmatising, often becoming the daily currency of abusive playground language. For the child, the world will provide a lasting challenge to the understanding and affirmation of self and identity.

Adjusting to the news that a child is different

Parenthood is a major point of transition (Busfield, 1987; and see Chapter 7) following the birth of the first child. A much greater adaptation has to take place when parents are told or suspect that their child has learning disabilities. Reactions can accommodate a range of responses including feelings of isolation, an identification with the particular or special qualities of their child, or indeed cause families to separate or reconstruct themselves in an attempt to adjust to a new life experience. At such a time, early intervention by a range of professionals might be appropriate (Simeonnson & Bailey, 1986).

The necessary adjustment made by lone parents bringing up a disabled child in particular is difficult, because lone parenthood itself embraces a time of tension and uncertainty. Since social attitudes towards such status remain ambivalent, professionals need to be aware of the support needed by the more isolated families in the community. An increasing number of studies informs our knowledge of how single parents, mainly mothers, cope: in an overall sense (e.g. Finer Report, 1974; Silva & Smart, 1998), financially (e.g. Burghes, 1994), and compared with two-parent families (e.g. Maclean & Eekelaar, 1997). A smaller output focuses specifically on lone mothers of children with learning disabilities (e.g. Cigno with Burke, 1997). We shall return to the peculiar situation of lone mothers in Chapters 4 and 5.

Grief and loss are common feelings experienced by parents who face, for the first time, the task of caring for a child with disabilities (Pollack & Stewart, 1997). One parent expressed his sense of grief as well as duty after his daughter was diagnosed as having 'developmental delay':

> 'She's our daughter and we should look after her. Knowing about "normal" children does not help you to understand her needs'

> (father of nine-year-old Lucy).

Parents have to adjust their expectations which might, for instance, be that their child will pass examinations at school and go to university, become an athlete or simply be an 'ordinary' son or daughter who will grow up to live independently and marry. Instead, they have to ask basic questions of professionals, such as, will he learn to walk or feed himself? Will he be able to go to school? The transitional passage which has to be followed is, therefore, considerable.

CASE EXAMPLE: Debbie

Debbie is a Down's child. Both parents agreed that the mother should not be tested during pregnancy for the condition (the mother was over 35) because they believed that they would accept their child whether born disabled or not. The consultant paediatrician informed the parents of the child's condition at midnight following her birth. The parents were impressed with his concern and willingness to be helpful.

Nevertheless, the family had difficulty in coming to terms with having a Down's child. In particular, the father said that it was hard to accept a 'handicapped' child. He spoke of his 'initial resistance' towards children with learning disabilities and of the struggle to change his attitudes and learn to accept the child that was now his. Both partners found support in one another, but discovered that their intellectual acceptance of a statistically possible Down's child was not the same as the reality. Eventually they felt that they could love all their children equally. Even so, the reality of their child's intellectual impairment combined with physical differences were hard to accept. The probability that Debbie could be involved in an executive capacity in the family's commercial business seemed remote. The plans they had for their unborn child were substituted by concerns to safeguard her future within a protective family environment.

Comment

In this example, there was no delay in informing parents of their child's condition, diagnosed immediately following her birth. However, the diagnosis itself did not convey the degree of learning disability which the child might experience, only that the condition itself was detectable and permanent. In fact, it would have been detectable during pregnancy had the parents wished to have tests. Their guiding belief, however, was that they would accept their child, whatever might happen. This belief was put to the test after Debbie's birth, as they struggled with their feelings, hopes and fears about impending changes to their family life.

The issue with prenatal detection is that parents then face a dilemma: go ahead or terminate the pregnancy. These are literally life and death issues for the baby, reflecting individual attitudes and values regarding abortion, people with disabilities generally and one's own family in particular (see also Chapter 8). This family thought that acceptance of a Down's child would not present a problem to their ability to love their child; it did, but now the child is loved for herself. Outcomes for the child and family cannot be predicted. These are serious and unanswerable matters; certainty of one's own *a priori* beliefs is no guarantee of actual feelings and behaviours in real-life situations.

The issue for doctors at the time of diagnosis is how much information is provided by the diagnosis procedure, what significance does the test result have, and how should any interpretation of these be conveyed to the parents. Not all Down's children are the same, intellectually or physically, and in that regard are like everyone else, so the child has to be valued equally, whether 'high' or 'low grade' intelligence within the Down's range. Again, the medical diagnosis is a label only, and can only predict the child's future life chances within broad, and perhaps unhelpful, parameters. These limits are present in the majority of situations involving a child with learning disabilities and point to the importance of considering both medical and social models of disability.

Vulnerability

A feature common to the experience of people with learning disabilities is that they are to some degree vulnerable to the influence of others throughout their lives and, depending on the severity of impairment, might only be able to lead a quality life if offered some form of protection and support. In early childhood, this protection may be available only from those with personal responsibility, usually parents (Burke & Cigno, 1996). One parent expressed this sense of vulnerability to us:

> 'Everyone who meets Sarah likes her, but it only takes someone to say, "come with me", and she'd go off with them and not question why'

> (mother of 13-year-old).

The difficulty with considering how an intellectual impairment affects an individual is that it is not uncommon for secondary and additional difficulties to result from or be initiated by the primary condition: the example of Sarah is indicative of the lack of awareness of risk to herself in the presence of strangers. This represents a risk which she is unable to grasp. Awareness training programmes, while necessary and useful, might not be able to ensure that the necessary caution is internalised. With many children, constant reinforcement of safe behaviour is necessary.

In part, the consequence of delayed achievement within the normal stages of development is responsible for, but is not restricted to, just this lack of social awareness, and includes the impact of development delays, as in crawling, walking and speech, which then have an impact on other abilities such as reading skills, creativity and interactions with others (see Chapter 3). Such delays are further barriers for the child when the carer attempts to access resources appropriate to age-related interests. These delays, too, add to the child's need for protection from harm.

While the term 'learning disability' conveys the sense of impaired capacity to learn, the positive question of what learning actually does take place must also be addressed. Some sense of 'feeblemindedness' and helplessness stemming from the Mental Deficiency Act of 1913 remains. This sense of perpetual dependency conveys the idea of 'forever children'. Professionals, as we shall show later, need to be concerned with encouraging individuals to grow from childhood to adulthood, with a concentration on people's strengths rather than their weaknesses. Sutton (1994) puts this well in her advocacy of the use of social learning theory (discussed in more detail in Chapter 11), which is concerned with emphasising people's strengths rather than their deficits, as a positive framework for planning and intervening in social work and related contexts. Practitioners also need to be alert to situations where the carers may not be acting in the child's best interests, either through incapacity to cope with a disabled child or through lack of support.

Vulnerability due to incapacity or impairment can lead to overprotection by parents, who in doing so deny their child opportunities which help to minimise their identity as learning-disabled. Frude (1991) considers that overprotection leads to the secondary disadvantage of over-dependency. It can lead to an excess of concern for the child whose learning and social opportunities may be curtailed out of concern for their well-being. Craft & Brown (1994) comment on elderly parents' concern for their adult daughter who took part in rock climbing and abseiling when on an activity-based holiday. They later said, 'We would never have let her do that. It must be good for her' (p. 37): a kind of recognition that, through the best of intentions, they may have been denying their daughter life-enhancing experiences.

Vulnerability and overprotection are linked, since one may give rise to the other, yet underprotection places the child at risk. The difficulty is in getting the balance right, and here parents may well need the advice of professionals who can observe and assess actual and potential abilities in a more detached and objective way, evaluating the degree of vulnerability the child might experience either through an excess of protective care or lack of care. Either situation, though more clearly the latter, may constitute neglect or abuse (see section 47 of the Children Act 1989).

In Chapter 8, we consider further the differences between intervening to support or to protect; and what happens when private and public care settings – the family included – become the places where the child and young person are at risk.

CASE EXAMPLE: **Martin**

Martin is the younger of two children. He is 12 and his sister 18. He was diagnosed as having cerebral palsy following a brain scan at eight months old after concerns were expressed by his parents about his slow development. As he grew older, he needed physiotherapy to help him crawl. Later, his parents were shown how to use a frame to help him to walk. By the age of five he was fully ambulant.

Martin needs constant attention because he has little sense of danger and displays inappropriate behaviours. One night his mother awoke to the noise of rushing water. Martin had filled the bath with hot water and put his bedclothes into it. He was about to get into the bath himself. Doors in the house have to be latched at night to prevent Martin wandering about the house, thereby putting himself at risk while his parents sleep.

Comment

This case illustrates the fact that children with a learning disability are vulnerable if they cannot anticipate danger or understand that their actions might lead to harm. This is true for all children to some degree, but generally children learn as they grow older which hazards to avoid and how to associate dangerous situations with harmful consequences. For instance, most 12-year-old children would not get into a bath of scalding water or indeed put their bedclothes in the bath during the night!

Martin's vulnerability arises from his inability to associate cause with effect: hot water causes burns and blistering. Clearly, he is a danger to himself and others if not protected from gaining access to potentially dangerous objects, for many household objects are harmful if used inappropriately. Martin's parents have to anticipate danger on his behalf. For example, waving a broomstick about, as Martin sometimes does, could cause injury to another person. Such behaviour might be expected in a small child and preventive measures taken. The case of an active 12-year-old is a different matter. Martin's carers need to learn how to achieve a balance between allowing him freedom to experiment while at the same time creating reasonable boundaries to contain his behaviour.

Cerebral palsy is, of course, not necessarily associated with learning disability, as in Martin's case. Many cerebral palsied children are assessed as having normal or high intelligence. The prize-winning young Irish writer Christopher Nolan is an example of the latter case. The 1999 'see the person' poster campaign sponsored by the Department for Education and Employment was not without its critics. It aimed at a 'person first' approach to disability, challenging assumptions which we all make about, for example, a woman with cerebral palsy, or a man who is wheelchair-bound.

The impact of the child on the carer

We have made the point that, while children with disabilities share much in common, each child possesses different characteristics which influence the course of his or her life. Thus, while carers and other family members are major players in what happens to their child, the child in question in part directs present and future outcomes. Children are not merely passive recipients of care: influence is two-way.

Howard, for instance, is an outdoor, sports-loving Down's child. He likes the open air and spends much of his out-of-school time at his grandparents' farm, where he helps to look after the animals. His mother has therefore investigated which sports competitions he can enter, as well as encouraging him to learn to swim and to ride. These activities are becoming the focus for his holidays. He has also given his family ideas for his future through his expressed wish to 'work with animals'. His mother is collecting information about work in farming communities, including those which cater specially for learning-disabled people.

Conclusion

While we have recognised that 'learning disability' is a term which replaced 'mental handicap' and is intended to be less stigmatising than the latter, we accept that the utility of any label should be judged on its ability to assist in a particular way those it is designed to identify. Families do not always understand or use these terms, although the case examples aim to illustrate how families come to realise that their child is different. Because families know their children and do not treat them as objects of concern or pathological interest, an individual and personal view is the result of knowing one's own child and what is best for him or her. Initial reactions to disabilities, such as shock, are demonstrated by the case of Debbie, but her case also shows how these were overcome as both parents got to know their child as a unique individual.

Issues – not necessarily problems – for families often concern their acceptance and protection of their vulnerable child, their need to learn to seek help when needed and not to feel isolated and different from other families. Their acceptance of their child may continue to contain ambivalence as family members struggle to adjust their expectations and 'do the right thing'. Professional help can guide parents through the difficult periods of readjustment that are needed. It is also a statutory duty under current child-related legislation.

Families of children with learning disabilities may need help in letting the child go. This is a healthy step towards the possibility of future independence (see the case of Kevin, Chapter 7). Parents occasionally have to learn that others can help and that their child can at some level be involved in choices. Indeed, all family members benefit by using services rather than withdrawing from what may seem like a hostile world. If this withdrawal is not to continue through life, families must learn to adjust to disability, as some degree of independence for their child is accommodated, and change is achieved while difficulties are faced, even overcome. Nevertheless, an awareness of the vulnerability of the disabled child from over- or underprotection is a main theme for children, families and professionals, and one which will recur throughout the book.

Chapter 3

Learning Disabilities and Child Development

Peter Randall

'And the first step, as you know, is always what matters most, particularly when we are dealing with those who are young and tender'

(Plato, 428–348 BC).

With its roots based firmly in the earliest events of child development, the study of learning disabilities has implications for our understanding of human potential throughout all its normal and abnormal manifestations. The vastly expanding knowledge base has led society from a ruthless segregationist philosophy encapsulated within the concept of 'mental subnormality' to the less restrictive concept of 'learning disabilities' which through the processes of inclusion and empowerment has become community rather than medical property (see also Chapter 1). Whereas at one time there were rigid classifications of those whose learning was below the norm, now we find a conflated spectrum of different levels of intellectual delays, adult dependence and developmental disorders subsumed under the generic term 'learning disabilities' of which the community is more likely to take ownership.

Parents want to know about causes, to learn why their children are learning-disabled. Often there is only confusion for them as the aetiological approach to learning disabilities has identified more than 200 known causes, ranging through infections and intoxications, trauma or physical agency, metabolism or nutrition, gross brain damage, unknown prenatal influence, chromosomal abnormality, conditions originating in perinatal period (e.g. prematurity and postmaturity), psychiatric disorder, environmental influences (including psychosocial disadvantage or sensory deprivation) and other conditions such as sensory defects (see, for example, Simonoff *et al.*, 1996). In general, those children with the most severe difficulties are shown fairly early on in life, if not at birth, to have organic aetiological diagnoses. For the most part, their development is found to be restricted from infancy onwards and every manifestation of abnormality affects loving parents as severely now as ever (Randall & Parker, 1999).

Over the last 25 years there have been many advances in the educational and behavioural technologies available for working with people with learning disabilities as they learn to develop life skills. In particular, innovations in behavioural strategies (e.g. Yule & Carr, 1987) have allowed sophisticated interventions to become a standard feature of most joint clinical and educational programmes. Thus, detailed methods for assisting parents to become the trainers of their own children (e.g. Bernal, 1984; Baker *et al.*, 1991) can be skilfully woven into highly structured individual education programmes such as the Portage material (White & Cameron, 1987). These programmes routinely use task analysis, shaping procedures and modelling, all delivered interestingly to the children with severe learning disabilities because there is a clear understanding of the practice of reinforcement schedules.

As welcome as these advances are for assisting people with learning disabilities, the biggest change in promoting their welfare within the community has little to do with strategic programmes. It would not matter how successfully educationalists and others laboured to assist children and young people with learning difficulties to reach levels of achievements unheard of only a few decades ago, if negative attitudes in society at large meant that their inclusion within the community was impossible. In the author's opinion the change in society's attitude towards people with learning difficulties ultimately has had the most pervasive and liberating impact on their lives.

Part of the shift in attitudes is illustrated by the changes in terminology that have occurred (see Chapter 5). Unpleasant and outmoded terms like 'educationally subnormal' and 'mental retardates' became socially unacceptable and followed older classifications such as 'imbeciles' and 'idiots' into history. However, more fundamentally, perceptions of people with learning disabilities gradually altered. They were seen increasingly as citizens who had rights to belong fully to society and to acquire the skills needed to have as much control over their lives and opportunities as possible. In short, these changes in attitude put their empowerment on the social agenda.

Similarities of developmental processes and needs

Much of this vital attitudinal shift has occurred because it is recognised that people with learning disabilities share very similar motivations, joys, anxieties and preferences as those without. Whilst still children, it is evident that those with learning disabilities follow patterns of development that are very similar to children whose development is unfettered; their skills may be acquired more slowly and some may have specific deficits or developmental disorders (for example, autism), but in general their progression is familiar.

CASE EXAMPLE: **Carey**

Carey is seven years old; she is sandwiched between her six- and eight-year-old brothers. One of her greatest joys is to sit between them in the back of the family car and play a variety of the 'I Spy' game. When one of them spots a selected object they all point at it and laugh delightedly.

Carey loves also to lie on the living-room floor with the two boys and watch *The Simpsons* cartoons. As often as not they end up in a giggly rough and tumble.

In these and countless other ways Carey displays her normality and zest for life alongside her brothers. At their ages at least they do not care that Carey's learning and physical disabilities restrict her 'I Spy' game to simple object recognition and eye pointing only, or that her appreciation of the cartoons is limited to enjoyment of the movement and bright colours. They know her so well that the differences in her development count for much less than the similarities.

The jigsaw puzzle of human development

As anyone who knows children and young people well, particularly their parents, human beings do not develop in discrete chunks. Although particular skills may exist in isolation to greater or lesser degrees of advancement, their interaction is complex, like a jigsaw puzzle, the whole being greater than the sum of its parts. Attempts made to extract specific areas of development from the overall and integrated functioning of human beings may be necessary for assessment and research purposes, but may detract from a holistic understanding of human development.

Nevertheless, it would be impossible to conceptualise the nature of learning disabilities without making some attempt to understand areas of strengths and weaknesses. Typically, the study of human development has endeavoured to conceptualise integrated functioning in terms of three broad varieties of personal characteristics and growth. In relation to learning disabilities, the area of greatest impact is on the domain of cognitive–intellectual development. This includes perception, language, problem-solving, thinking skills, memory and educational achievement. This will, of course, also have an effect on the other two areas. Of these the physical–motor domain encompasses motor skills coordination, size, strength, physical health as well as body build. The last domain, personal–social, is concerned with social skills, emotional adjustment, temperament, moral awareness and social behaviour.

The deficiencies of such a segregation are obvious in a number of ways. For example, children's development of thinking and reasoning will certainly influence the way in which they learn to use their bodies within the physical–motor domain. If their understanding of how their bodies can be put to use in terms of physical activity is limited, then it is quite likely that their play skills will not develop efficiently, and this would have a direct impact on the development of peer relations in the personal-social domain. Progress in one area generally affects progress in the others; conversely, deficits in one may impact on the rest. For example, children who are malnourished cannot learn effectively and those with low self-esteem gain little confidence in the use of their intellectual skills. Children who are emotionally abused and neglected show such damage to the personal–social domain that they find it hard to learn directly from others (e.g. through imitation) so that the cognitive–intellectual domain is not facilitated (Iwaniec, 1995).

Human development does not, of course, follow some genetic blueprint. It is fashioned within environmental influences as well. For many years it has been recognised that children's development is influenced by parents and other individuals as social forces providing opportunities and models for learning and social interaction (see, for example, Schaffer, 1971; Bijou, 1976; Sutton, 1999). In turn, the development of a child will influence relevant others within his or her immediate environment such that the behaviour of parents, siblings, teachers and peers may all be modified by the way in which a child develops. The circularity of cause and effect resounds throughout the course of human development to create individuals with unique characteristics and adaptability.

Developmental needs

This crude division of child development into the three domains is useful in relation to the identification of changing needs as children progress. In particular the similarities between the learning-disabled and non-learning-disabled child populations are revealed most strongly in terms of the similar needs that they have as they move through the stages of infancy from birth to a developmental age of about six years. A useful delineation of these developmental differences has been provided by Donohue-Colletta (1992) for three age groups, as Table 3.1 shows.

Table 3.1   Child development needs to age six years.

Infants (birth to one year) need:

Protection from physical danger
Adequate nutrition
Adequate health care
Adults with whom to form attachments
Adults who can understand and respond to their signals
Things to look at, touch, hear, smell and taste
Opportunities to explore the world
Appropriate language stimulation

Infants (developmentally one to three years of age) need all the above and:
Support in acquiring new motor, language and thinking skills
A chance to develop appropriate independence behaviours
Assistance in learning how to control their own behaviour
Opportunities to begin learning to care for themselves
Regular daily opportunities for play with a variety of objects/people
   (including one or more familiar adults)

Children (developmentally three to six years of age, and over) require the above and:
Opportunities to develop fine motor skills
Encouragement of language through talking, reading, singing
Activities to develop a positive sense of mastery
Opportunities to begin the development of cooperation, helping, sharing
Education in respect of pre-writing and pre-reading skills

Although Table 3.1 concerns sequential development from birth, development begins prenatally and learning effectively begins at birth. Therefore, attention to the developmental and learning needs of all children should begin with pre- and postnatal interventions and be continued thereafter into adequate pre-school education.

It is axiomatic that the wide variety of inputs required to support children's growth and development all require someone enthusiastic to interact with the children. Dedicated parents and teachers are as necessary to the non-learning-disabled population as to any other, irrespective of their intellectual status. Dedication is not enough, however; there must also be an awareness of the processes involved in the promotion of child development, whether or not there is a learning disability. It is profitable to remind ourselves that there are certain vital issues concerning child development as true for the 'normal' child as the one who has learning disabilities. Developing pre-school intervention programmes requires an understanding of this holistic development; and this means paying attention to health, emotional and physical security and nutrition, as well as cognitive and socio-emotional characteristics.

Normally development proceeds in predictable stages (see Table 3.2) and the associated learning occurs in known sequences, albeit with considerable individual and social variation. Irrespective of their levels of intellectual impairment, educational and social strategies should accord with the children's growth pattern, not simply in terms of their cognitive efficiency, but also in respect of affective, perceptual and motor development. Whereas activities with young children should be developmentally challenging, there is no purpose in attempting learning that is beyond their current conceptual awareness; all children, be they learning-disabled or not, will not learn new skills effectively if they cannot integrate them through accommodation or assimilation with prior learning. Integrated interventions that promote developmentally appropriate learning across the board of child development are intrinsically more useful to all young children than those activities which stimulate only one sense or developmental area.

Development and learning occur continuously for all children as a result of their interacting with people and objects in their environment. The role of adults at home and school is to provide children with opportunities to work with concrete objects, to develop mastery through choice-making, by exploring objects and concepts, experimentation and discovery. In addition, all children need opportunities to interact with other children and adults in a safe environment that provides them with security, nurturance and acceptance. As a result, interventions must focus on the physical environment also with a view to making changes as necessary. This

Table 3.2 Normal language, motor and social developmental expectations (two to five years) (adapted from Bender & Valletutti, 1976).

Year	Language–expressive and receptive	Motor–gross and fine	Social skills
2	Demonstrates understanding of several action verbs Appears to listen to language Points to body parts when asked Uses two- to three-word sentences Uses personal pronouns (I, me, you) Asks for help Speaking vocabulary averages 20 to 40 words Asks 'what' type questions	Walks up and down stairs Runs; jumps (beginning stage) Kicks a large ball Builds six-block tower Turns pages in a book Strings 1-inch beads Drinks from a cup Uses spoon for feeding Removes pants (with assistance) Washes and dries hands (partially) Copies a vertical line	Engages in limited group play Does not like to share
3	Uses simple sentences Uses plurals Knows family name Obeys prepositional commands (on, in, under)	Stands on one foot Uses alternate feet going upstairs Rides tricycle Walks on tiptoes, walks in straight line Feeds self independently Unbuttons medium-size buttons Puts on and removes clothing (socks, shoes, underpants) Copies a circle Washes and dries hands	Shares toys Begins to interact with other children

4	Uses complete sentences Uses conjunctions Knows own age Knows simple analogies	Balances on one foot, hops Throws ball overhand Laces shoes Drinks with a straw Feeds self with a fork, brushes teeth Prints some capital letters Attempts to print own name Draws a man on request (crude)	Attempts cooperative play with other children Works well for praise Begins to obey rules Looks for attention Shares rather than grabs objects
5	Has comprehensible speech Solves simple verbal problems May recognise written name Recognises some of the alphabet	Walks downstairs alternating feet Hops, skips and balances Prints first name Draws recognisable man Buttons medium-size buttons Dresses self (except for small buttons)	Responds positively to suggestions Interacts with others Well poised (at times)

may involve freedom from abuse or domestic violence, increasing parental income, minimising health risks in the home as well as the community, enabling all the vital process factors that come with good schools and libraries, clean parks and people-friendly buildings together with the socio-political milieu which promotes unconditional positive regard for all people.

All children should be active participants in their own development through learning. It is the author's experience that, even among many educationalists, there is often a fundamental and mistaken belief that children develop because of teaching. This is not the reality of education: adults teach and hopefully children will learn as a result. It is the case, however, that learning (and associated development) involves the children's own construction of knowledge which is not the same thing as adults' imposition of information. The skills which are the basis of development improve with practice; this is particularly evident among the slower-learning population with developmental delay. It is important for infant children (and the developmentally young) to have opportunities to learn by doing, to be actively involved in problem-solving, and to formulate language and communication skills from their use (see, for example, Haskell & Barrett, 1993).

Encouraging participation of individuals with learning disabilities is not only meeting a need, it is an important strategy which facilitates their empowerment. The process of empowering people with learning disabilities has required a completely radical reconceptualisation of the problems presented by learning disabilities (Swift & Levin, 1987). This reinterpretation has led to a reversal of old assumptions that the problems created by learning disabilities lie not in the person, but in his or her relationship to the community. The roots of this significant attitudinal change are to be found in Wolfenberger's (1972) concept of normalisation translated over a 15-year period into an ecological model. This has enabled intervention to move away from simple nursing and caring about physical welfare towards the alteration of the individual's relationship with their environment so that they have enhanced opportunities to gain as much control as possible over their own lives.

Range of learning disabilities

It is clear that there is a gradation of severity among the population with learning disabilities. Those who are at the most severe end of the continuum are more likely to have an organic aetiology and show developmental disorders such as autism. It is helpful to consider an operational definition of learning disability which enables parents and professionals to begin to define severity and thus structure effective responses to individuals. An examination of the literature indicates a wide disparity of viewpoints (see Chapter 1). The term 'learning disabilities' as used in the UK refers to people who have an intellectual impairment that prevents them from learning at a normal rate. The same term in the US refers to individuals who are not intellectually impaired but still have difficulties with some aspects of learning. Neither interpretation is to be confused with the educational use of the term 'specific learning difficulties' of which 'dyslexia' is the most commonly used lay term.

A definition given by Grossman (1983) encapsulates this understanding in respect of those people who have a:

> '... significantly subaverage general intellectual functioning resulting in or associated with concurrent impairments in adaptive behaviour, and manifested during the developmental period'

> (p. 11).

It is important to understand what is meant by 'impairment in adaptive behaviour' from the preceding definition. Grossman (1983) refers to this as:

> '... significant limitations in an individual's effectiveness in meeting the standards of maturation, learning, personal independence, and/or social responsibility that are expected for his or her age level and cultural group'

> (p. 11).

In diagnostic terms, individuals with learning disabilities must show significantly below average intellectual functioning (at or below second percentile) and also impairment in their adaptive behaviour before the age of 18 years.

Informing parents of developmental stages

It helps some parents to be told at what stages and in what order important developmental milestones are normally reached. Child development does have a clear pathway towards independence that is not fixed or invariable but is nevertheless highly predictable. The pre-school years show a more clearly defined pathway of development than at any other time in life (for example, the ageing process) and this is tied fairly closely to chronological age. Although children with learning disabilities go through the stages of development as far as their intellectual deficits allow, their developmental behaviours are, in the author's clinical experience, far less crisply defined than for those children who develop at a normal rate. Many of the more profoundly disabled children will not progress far along the pathway, remaining all their lives within the earliest stages of development (see Table 3.2).

An understanding of the normal developmental sequence can be very helpful in assisting parents to realise why mastery of particular skills is necessary before new ones can be acquired. Parents can understand then why their child cannot 'run before they can walk'.

The author has used Table 3.2 when working with many parents. They feel assisted by being shown approximately where their child is and what stages have been achieved to get there. Such explanations are always given, however, with the warning that there is no hard and fast progression; not all children will follow the sequence exactly.

Learning disabilities and developmental prognosis

Despite the movement away from 'medical model' (see Chapter 1) determinations of learning disabilities, the best researched gradation of learning disabilities is frequently decided by the performance of individuals on standardised tests of intellectual ability (WHO, 1992). These tests generally give results as intelligence quotients (IQ). It must be remembered that such results are not fixed and invariable and many factors influence how well or badly individuals may perform at the time of being tested, as the case of Douglas demonstrates in Chapter 7. These factors include tiredness, stress, concentration span and how well they get on with the person doing the testing. Neverthless, the results are of significant prognostic value and the gradations made possible by them are given below.

Mild (IQ 50–69)

People with mild learning disabilities acquire language normally but more slowly than the population without difficulties. A significant majority achieve sufficient speech and language for all everyday purposes, to hold conversations and to make their needs known.

Their self-help skills eventually offer them full independence in relation to the self-care activities of eating, washing, dressing, bowel and bladder control as well as most practical and domestic skills. Although their rate of development is slower than normal it does follow normal stages of progression.

Their biggest difficulties occur in relation to academic skills; problems in the acquisition of literacy and numeracy are often the first definite signs of their learning disabilities. Their academic problems can be significantly lessened by a well-differentiated and closely structured curriculum content and process which is often carried on beyond the age of compulsory education into further education and training settings.

Most people with mild difficulties are potentially capable of routine unskilled work that makes few demands on academic abilities. Unskilled or semi-skilled manual work is a reasonable aspiration for most and they may pursue this consistently well through to normal retirement age.

In community settings where the social cultural context does not require much by the way of academic achievement, their mild learning disabilities do not generally present a problem. Where, however, there is noticeable emotional and sociable immaturity, the individual with mild learning disabilities may find the complexities of marriage, parenting and other intense relationships too challenging. The lower the IQ of the individual, the more likely problems of neglect are to occur in respect of their children and this probability rises with every child in his or her care. Research demonstrates that most people at this level of ability experience serious problems in their role as parents (e.g. Whitman & Accardo, 1993). Often, the determination of the parent as having a low IQ is used as a prime determinant of their projected ability to cope with the needs of babies and young children. Booth & Booth (1993) suggest that there is a bias held by professionals against parents with learning disabilities. They conclude that service providers fail to overcome this bias such that there is insufficient consideration about how best they can enable the citizenship rights of these parents as well as protect the welfare of their children. It must also be noted that some researchers have determined that the way parents with learning disabilities are treated by society also affects their parenting style independently of the extent of their learning disability (Tymchuk & Feldman, 1991). It is the case, however, that parents with learning disabilities can be trained to be effective parents given the right circumstances and support (e.g. Bakken *et al.*, 1993). Sheerin (1998) presents a detailed review of the literature and concludes that parents with learning disablilites are likely to experience problems in the absence of proper social supports, including parent education. Sheerin also points out that such assistance is given to parents with learning disabilities only when their children have been found to be at risk, when it is too late to avoid 'significant' harm.

Many people with learning disabilities tend also to show poor functional performance in a variety of areas that impact directly on their parenting skills (Mulhall, 1989; Baldwin *et al.*, 1991). Such difficulties typically include the failure to establish consistent domestic routines, problems with social communication, memory and other cognitive weakness and a tendency to refer decision-making to other people. Such parents often find it hard to assert themselves against more dominant people and, in the author's experience, they are frequently unable to protect their children against harm from others. This difficulty is not, of course, restricted only to parents with learning disabilities; in fact it is important to remember that the majority of parents who are neglectful or abusive do not have learning disabilities (Iwaniec, 1995).

In general terms, the emotional, social and behavioural difficulties of people with mild learning disabilities and the treatment and support provision they need are more closely aligned to provisions used by people of normal ability than to the specific and complex problems associated with more severe forms of learning disabilities. Indeed one would expect this to be the case, as the majority of people with mild learning disabilities do not show specific organic aetiology.

Moderate (IQ 20–49)

The more severe the level of learning disabilities the more likely organic aetiology is to be found. People within these ranges are very slow to develop receptive and expressive language and frequently plateau at early stages of language development. Their rate of acquisition of motor skills and self-care/independence skills is also significantly slower and only a small proportion learn any functional literacy and numeracy skills. Educational programmes making use of behavioural principles such as task analysis, shaping and modelling enable them to develop their potential for learning and to acquire basic independence skills.

As adults, they are usually able to complete simple practical work once the tasks are broken down finely and carefully structured. Skill supervision is inevitably required, and even as adults there will be a moderate to high level of dependency on others. Most will need supervision throughout life as completely independent living is rarely achieved.

This rather restricting picture is mitigated to a significant extent, however, by the fact that most are mobile and physically active and many show sufficient social development to engage in sociable activities with other people, communicate their needs and demonstrate their preferences.

Organic aetiology is frequently identified in this group and childhood autism or other pervasive developmental disorders are not uncommon. Such comorbidity makes the educational and developmental process much more difficult and invariably has a significant impact on the type of management needed. Neurological disabilities (e.g. epilepsy) as well as physical (e.g. cerebral palsy) are common amongst this group, who unfortunately also show much higher rates of psychiatric disorder than the non-learning-disabled population.

Profound (IQ below 20)

This individual is severely limited in his or her ability to understand normal interactions or comply with requests, make his or her needs known and engage socially within the family or community. Frequently, such individuals show severe restrictions of mobility and movement in general. Often they have sensory deficits and remain incontinent of bowel and bladder. They have exceptionally high adult dependency and require constant help and supervision for life. Pervasive developmental disorders such as atypical autism are present in many cases, making more difficult the tasks of parents and teachers.

Education and learning disabilities

For educational purposes children in the UK with learning disabilities are normally classified along a continuum with *moderate learning difficulties* at one end and *profound and multiple learning difficulties* at the other. In between are children with *severe learning difficulties* (SLD). Those with the most serious conditions show high adult dependency and will not achieve full independence in adult life whereas those with only mild to moderate learning problems are expected to access a normal curriculum modified to meet their individual needs. It is important to understand that this classification is needs-led rather than tied strictly to measurement on intellectual tests.

Clearly the educational process has much to contribute to the empowerment of people with learning disabilities. Moreover, their rights to an appropriate education are enshrined in law. With regard to education legislation, the special educational needs of children and young people with learning disabilities are defined and protected by a Code of Practice (Department of Education, 1994) which is a vitally important outcome of the 1993 Education Act. This Act required the Secretary of State to issue such a code of practice giving guidance to local educational authorities and the governing bodies of all maintained schools concerning their responsibility towards children with special educational needs (SEN). This Code of Practice has been in operation since 1 September 1994 and even though the 1993 Act has been superseded by the 1996 Education Act, the latter has not made any significant difference to the duties that LEAs and the schools are under in respect of pupils with SEN. Thus, all those to whom the Code applies (LEAs and their offices, school governors, head-teachers, classteacher, educational psychologists and others) have a statutory duty to take account of it; they cannot ignore it.

Among many other requirements, the Code places duties upon LEAs to identify children with SEN and involve their parents by seeking views and observations about their children as well as opinions about the provision needed.

Paragraphs 3:55 to 3:59 respectively of the Code of Practice deal with the special educational needs of children with learning difficulties. It is important to know that educationalists prefer to use the term 'learning difficulties' rather than 'learning disabilities'. This is largely a consequence of the evidence received by the Warnock Committee (Warnock Report, 1979) in relation to preferred nomenclature among the population having impaired learning. Where a pupil has a particular form of learning difficulty, such as 'dyslexia', then he or she is referred to as having 'specific learning difficulties'. The Code of Practice makes clear that children with general learning difficulties will show a general level of academic achievement significantly below that of their peers. It states that they will show difficulty in acquiring basic literacy and numeracy skills and many among them will also have significant speech and language problems. The Code recognises also that such children may have problems in learning normal social skills and so show signs of poor adjustment, as well as emotional or behavioural problems.

Where children have severe or profound or multiple learning difficulties, the Code states that the LEA should be able to utilise a considerable body of existing knowledge from other services such as child health and social services. The basis of this belief is that these agencies may well have been involved with the child and his or her family from an early stage. Such children are expected to have additional secondary disabilities (e.g. physical, sensory, emotional, behavioural). The Code requires that assessment arrangements must take these into account. In all cases, however, the social services department will be asked to provide any information it may have about the child and his or her family. Normally there is little or no information but, on occasions, the social services department may combine assessment of children 'in need' under schedule 17 of the Children Act 1989 with statutory assessment under the 1996 Education Act.

The breadth of assessment that LEA schools undertake with children with learning difficulties is considerable as defined in paragraph 3:57 of the Code of Practice. For example, the LEA must seek clear, recorded evidence of a number of factors which may impinge directly on academic attainment. This includes evidence that:

(1) The child is not benefiting from working on material relevant to the key stage appropriate to his or her age from within the National Curriculum.

(2) The child is working at a level significantly below his or her peers and falling progressively behind these peers in relation to the National Curriculum core subjects.

(3) Impaired social interactions or communication or 'a significantly restricted repertoire of activities, interests and imaginative development' are present.

(4) The child has significant problems at home or within family circumstances, particularly in relation to his or her attendance record.

(5) There exist emotional or behavioural difficulties which may be indicated by recorded examples of withdrawn or disruptive behaviour; persistently poor attention control; difficulties in securing and maintaining good peer relations and any other evidence of a delay in the development of life and social skills.

(6)   Medical or social problems have led to assessments or interventions by child health or social services.

Where the balance of this recorded evidence indicates that the
learning difficulties are significant and/or complex, have not
responded to relevant and consistent measures taken by the school
and other agencies involved, and may require special educational
provision that is not within the resources of the school, then the LEA
must consider making a statutory assessment of the child's special
educational needs under the 1996 Education Act.

Such an assessment will involve detailed reports from a minimum
of three professionals: teachers, doctors and educational psychologists. Others may also be involved (e.g. speech and language
therapists, physiotherapists, social workers) depending on the nature of the special educational needs. In addition, the law requires
that the advice and opinions of the parents are actively sought.

It is, however, the educational psychologist who is most likely to be
involved in determining the level of learning disability. These psychologists are skilled in educational and developmental psychology;
their expertise lies in profiling the strengths and weaknesses of pupils
with special educational needs and relating this profile to educational
provision and programmes. To do this they have to work closely with
parents and do their best to answer questions and to explain the
meaning of the observations that the parents make.

When contributing to statutory assessments, educational psychologists are bound by the Code of Practice to address the wide
range of factors that affect children's functioning. These include
thinking and reasoning abilities; communication skills; perceptual
skills; self-help and personal and social skills; the children's
approach to learning and the attitudes they have in respect of the
learning process as well as their educational attainments. In addition, the psychologists should take careful note of the children's self-
image, interest and behaviour. Where the children have been
involved with other psychologists (e.g. clinical psychologists) the
educational psychologist must liaise with them and incorporate the
information they have.

In the context of this chapter, however, the liaison that educational psychologists should have with parents is of particular
relevance. In the author's experience, many ask questions about
their children's development long before they start school. Unfortunately they may not have received a satisfactory response to their
questions or may have been brushed off with platitudes concerning

'late development' (Randall & Parker, 1999). The following questions, frequently asked by parents, may indicate the presence of learning disabilities.

Why does he knock into his building bricks, bump into doors, fall out of his chair and bang into his friends and family?
Parents are often referring here to a constellation of difficulties arising from:

- inability to 'steer' his body around his physical environment
- delayed depth perception
- delayed visual motor coordination
- toe walking or other immature gait.

These difficulties are common among the population of ambulant pre-school children who have mild learning disabilities but whose late-maturing mobility skills have been particularly noted. Sometimes they have developmental coordination disorder (dyspraxia) as well as learning disabilities.

Why can't she concentrate on anything – why does she flit from one thing to another?
This question indicates that parents may be observing:

- distractibility or a delay in the process whereby a child learns to attend selectively to stimuli
- delay in the development of attention control
- immaturity resulting in impulsivity
- hyperactivity resulting from the failure to develop age-appropriate inhibitory controls on behaviour
- perseveration, often a means for the child with delay to rehearse cause and effect relationships until they can reliably predict them.

Poor attention control is often a significant problem for children with learning disabilities. They cannot process information well enough at the early stages of their development to be able to sift what is important from the background 'noise'. In addition, their concentration span is limited and, as a result, learning materials have to be presented in short bursts once their extraneous activity has been brought to an end.

He seems to understand most things I say to him, but why can't he express himself well like his brother and sister could at the same age?'
What is being observed may be:

- delayed speech
- limited vocabulary
- general language delay.

The parent may well be overestimating the child's understanding of language or underestimating the amount of non-verbal cues unknowingly given by them that assist understanding; the delay in speech output is, however, much more noticeable, particularly when there are previous children in the family to make comparisons with.

She looks at everything but doesn't seem to see anything in particular; why don't things seem to make much of an impact on her?
A wide range of delayed intellectual skills may be responsible for:

- a delay in distinguishing shapes and colours
- poorly developed memory, creating difficulty in remembering what is seen
- immature sequencing skills such that the child has difficulty in remembering the order in which he or she sees and hears events
- a delay in the growth of concept formation and association, making it hard for the child to make sense of new experiences.

This kind of observation is generally about the core intellectual deficit right at the heart of learning disabilities; the parent is noticing the difficulty the child has in assimilating the environmental stimuli that normally promote age-appropriate learning. Failing to make sense of what is seen is often more noticeable to parents than failing to make sense of what is heard.

He's four years old but acts much younger: why?
Of all the questions asked, this is the one that is a particularly strong indicator of learning disabilities. The child may show:

- immature behaviour/appearance
- immature speech
- immature coordination/movement
- selection of solitary play with toys associated with younger children and/or choice of younger playmates
- failure to understand the 'rules' of cooperative play
- immature choice and use of toys.

Here the parent is noticing that the personal–social presentation of their child is substantially below the age norm. Often mistaking the behaviour as naughtiness or attention-seeking, parents need assistance to understand that their child has difficulty in learning apparently simple lessons which are, in fact, very complex rules about how to relate to others.

He looks at me really intently, and listens well, but why doesn't it seem to sink in?
The parent is observing that the child has problems with the reception and comprehension of language and that the ability to translate verbal directions into appropriate behaviour is not developing or is developing only slowly: There are:

- problems understanding what he or she hears
- difficulties remembering what he or she hears
- problems remembering sequences of sounds
- difficulties following simple directions because there is a delay in the mediation of behaviour by language.

This is another aspect of the cognitive–intellectual difficulties that characterise the population with learning disabilities. Working memory and speed of information processing are not adequate to handle the pace and complexity of stimulus input and the 'message' becomes fragmented and confusing.

She overreacts to everything – why does she behave like a terrible two?
The parent is observing:

- extremely uncontrolled emotional responses to minor provocations
- perseverated challenging behaviours from infancy (temper tantrums)
- the impact of faulty learning arising from modelling behaviour on poorly behaved or younger children.

This is a reflection of delay in social learning which, under normal circumstances, would enable the child to defer self-gratification gradually and begin to lose the overwhelming egocentricity that characterises the infant's response to his or her social environment.

Why can't he get things together right when I spend so much more time and energy helping him than I do my other children?
The parent observes:

- disorganised movements
- disorganised language when describing plans
- poor or absent goal-planning.

These questions go right to the core of learning disabilities. The central intellectual impairment prevents development of organisational skills at the normal rate. This leaves the child confused about the sequencing of tasks and chaining together of simple behaviours to achieve a more complex goal.

Conclusion

Changes in attitude to people with learning disabilities have coincided with a burgeoning in our understanding of strategies for their empowerment. Helping many young people with learning disabilities to enter citizenship as fully as possible has become a reality that contrasts starkly with the segregation that was practised previously.

In part, this has come about because society has recognised that there are more similarities than there are differences between the learning-disabled and non-learning-disabled populations. This recognition has encouraged the right of parents to take part with professionals in furthering their children's development. The professional–parent relationship is made more valuable when care is taken to ensure that parents have a good understanding of the process and sequences of child development. This helps parents make better use of training strategies and also provides them with a clearer prognosis to plan for. They are enabled to make more informed choices and better use of resources.

Chapter 4

Family Matters: Informal Support

In this chapter, we focus on the importance of the family itself in caring for children with learning disabilities. We examine the impact of exceptional strains and stresses on families and the ways in which family responses can be dysfunctional.

Although family patterns change over time and between cultures, the family remains pivotal in the care of dependent members, whether child or adult. Its underlying values may be hotly contested and criticised, particularly if appearing to sanction mainly white, middle-class values. Sometimes unconscious endorsements of a particular familial type will be regarded as inherently oppressive (Dominelli, 1997), especially by those who lament its change and disapprove of any newly evolving family structures (see, for example, Beck & Beck-Gernsheim, 1995). The movement from 'extended' family structures to what is usually described as 'nuclear' families has been apparent for many years; there is still considerable variety among ethnic groups in the extent of this change. Smart & Neale (1999), for example, examine the dangers of family fragmentation and consider the role of the state in unifying the family in the late twentieth century. Furthermore, as we shall see in the discussion of family networks, even in relation to 'nuclear' families there are still important connections with other kin. Contemporary family patterns in the UK today are diverse, even within the majority cultures.

The family

The modern family usually consists of partners (not necessarily married) and their dependent children: in other words, a unit composed of two parents and one, two or three children. Other family forms are on the increase, with a growing number of children being brought up by single parents (Burghes, 1994), in stepfamilies

(Gorell Barnes *et al.*, 1998) and in same-sex households (Tasker & Golombok, 1997), but an analysis of these situations is beyond the scope of this book. In this context, we note that the small amount of evidence so far available appears to indicate that the parents of children with learning disabilities are more likely to be married rather than cohabiting; although the number of single mothers is relatively high (Cigno with Burke, 1997). A further finding, with obvious and serious implications for lone mothers, is that the single most important source of support for parents was each other (Burke & Cigno, 1996). We cannot here consider the implications of these diverse patterns for the care of learning-disabled children, but we shall consider the effects of more tightly knit family structures in the way vulnerable members are supported.

The change of family composition to a smaller unit with greater mobility has meant that the extended family, as a possible source of help and support, is not necessarily available. The expectation of having at hand a very involved, extended family is no longer part of everyday family life in the post-industrial period. This means that visits to grandparents (who might be geographically remote) for support cannot be counted on due to the lower level of contact and involvement in family routine. It is not that larger or smaller families are better, only that smaller families tend to be more insular while larger ones, as might be expected, are more available and visible as sources of support. However, it does not follow that smaller family units are not adept at developing social relationships, rather that the immediate family base is restricted. Indeed, larger families nowadays might experience some form of isolation in their community and neighbourhood. What is clear is that the available source of support is less in evidence for small families who are either at a geographical distance from their relatives, or are without near relatives.

For most of us, in both our private and professional lives, it is not an uncommon experience to turn first to relatives, friends and neighbours to help resolve difficulties, and only to other services when these fail, particularly when problems are too vast or too complex to resolve by informal advice alone. How and when families seek help from formally organised sources of support is the subject of Chapter 5.

Friends, relatives and neighbours

Cooke & Lawton (1984) found from their research that families will, in fact, turn to friends, relatives and neighbours at times of crisis, although, somewhat surprisingly, nearly one-third of the families involved indicated that they did not have access to such an informal means of support. Our research, too, indicated that informal support was not available to all. Although the proportion was not as great as that found by Cooke & Lawton, the message is that some families lack help or advice from friends, relatives and neighbours.

We found (Burke & Cigno, 1995) that relatives were generally the major source of help for parents. Grandparents in particular often had strong attachments to their grandchildren, enabling parents to have some social life away from their predominantly caring responsibilities. Where this did not happen, or where there was contact but not support, parents tended to draw the distinction between the two. One parent expressed her relationship with her mother rather simply, saying, 'I see my mother but she's not a support for Alan' (reported in Burke & Cigno, 1995). This quote illustrates the differences that a child with learning disabilities brings to an otherwise 'normal' family, and the gulf which may then develop between parents and other relatives who fail to understand the additional stresses the family has to face.

Friends sometimes provided practical help, but were held onto with difficulty. One parent expressed this view:

'I often don't accept invitations to friends' homes because of Helen's behaviour – she picks things up, breaks ornaments'

(mother of nine-year-old Helen).

Where neighbours are concerned, families tell us that they have to work hard to create or maintain good relations. The following case example helps to illustrate how one family moved house to improve the availability of informal support networks, primarily from maternal grandparents.

CASE EXAMPLE: **Louise**

Louise is nine and has a younger sister, Jessica, aged six. At the age of three Louise had three epileptic fits and was admitted to hospital where she remained under sedation for five days. It was from this time that both parents suspected that she might have learning difficulties.

Louise is now fully ambulant but has little sense of danger. She would happily go off with anyone who asks her; her parents therefore say that she is at risk if left unattended. On a number of occasions, she has run out of the house into the street. Neighbours cannot be expected to 'watch out for her'. Louise needs constant attention from responsible adults: her parents, during the times when she is at home.

The family live in council property in a small seaside town. They moved to their present home to be nearer to Louise's and Jessica's maternal grandmother. Neighbours sometimes help with babysitting, grandparents are supportive, but partner support is the vital element in Louise's daily management.

Louise will remain at her special school where she is escorted daily on the school bus. Teachers at Louise's school are helpful but face-to-face contact is rare due to transport arrangements. The benefits of the recent house move are somewhat counteracted by the increased sense of isolation from school, which is now more distant, making school functions difficult to attend. Extended family support is thereby a much-felt need by Louise's parents, particularly during the summer holidays.

Comment

Louise lives in a typical, small, nuclear family. However, it is clearly the case that, given her needs, her parents chose to move to an area where they could rely on wider family support from Louise's grandmother. Neighbourhood support is also present and, like help from school, is highly valued. What is interesting to note is that continuous family and social support are valued more highly than support received from Louise's teachers, because they are not available during the summer holidays and are geographically distant in term-time. We noted in our research that teachers were often cited as being the most supportive professionals and the greatest source of help and advice, but, in this case, family help is clearly prized more highly, and this value guides decisions.

The need for continuous support is essential for this family, who find that mutual partner support is improved if supplemented with additional familial and local help. The role of professionals in such a case is to support the family in their choices and to be on hand should their needs change. Support from relatives, plus occasional babysitting from neighbours, have helped this family to manage their caring duties within their new home environment.

It is easier said than done for a parent to find adequate time for all the family when one member requires a large amount of special care.

Families with children with learning disabilities might inadvertently neglect other siblings, so in Louise's case, the needs of Jessica must also be considered (see Chapter 6). Such situations may lead to emotional neglect and the need for counselling or support groups for siblings, even when they are not identified as carers (Petr & Barney, 1993; Action for Children, 1995). Children like Jessica learn not to talk to others about having a disabled sister (or brother as the case may be), or indeed about the amount of caring they may be, or feel, obliged to do (Thompson, 1995). Powell & Ogle (1985) suggest that, apart from counselling and support services, siblings need information about disabilities, services, and what the future might hold both for their brother or sister who is disabled as well as for themselves.

Louise's family have, however, apparently found their own solutions to their need for support, and would be considered a functional family. They also have qualities of an extended family, given the availability of maternal grandparents following their house move. The importance of the family in providing support has underpinned social policy for many years and was a central plank in the concept of community care policies (Griffiths, 1988) and subsequent legislation (e.g. Nation Health Service and Community Care Act 1990; Carers (Recognition and Services) Act 1995).

Functional and dysfunctional families

Functional families may be defined as families who manage their day-to-day stresses. Dysfunctional ones do not, since they tend to be reactive rather than proactive to situations, a tendency which reduces their sense of being able to think through and problem-solve. Naturally, though, most families will figure somewhere between these two extremes. In addition, families often fluctuate between functional success and disruption. In the case of the family where there is a child with learning disabilities, parental reactions to the child might not always be consistent and helpful, such that stress builds up in the family and all members are adversely affected to the point of dysfunction. This simplified frame of reference is one that we find helpful when considering real situations.

The concept of function is described within systems theory by James & Wilson (1986), where it is used as a means for analysing the characteristics of the family. The helping professions are more usually concerned with families under stress, when coping mechanisms are challenged and weakened. The danger at these times is that such families will not adequately carry out their caring tasks: child care, providing meals and paying essential bills. Stress can be the result of not being able to adequately carry out routines necessary for daily living, or can precede it.

Families with children with learning disabilities often talk of being in a constant state of tension and crisis. As one mother commented:

> 'We are forever finding new obstacles to overcome. Necessary aids and equipment are not forthcoming, a change of teacher at school might cause Joseph additional distress, or the limited respite care we get is subject to another review ... probably cuts. We experience a constant strain on our emotions due to all this uncertainty'
>
> (mother of 13-year-old-boy with severe learning disabilities).

The way in which families manage can also be distributed on a continuum ranging from chaotic to rigid approaches to family organisation. At one extreme, the family barely reacts to problems and obstacles while at the other, it overreacts by engaging in frantic activity to try to overcome them. The first type of family may be drawn into a situation of neglect, and the second to crisis and breakdown.

The sense of belonging that engenders the family unit, whatever its size, is about the need for minimal care and support. Caring for a disabled child increases these needs, leading to stresses which expose the family to professional involvement. Risk of confrontation grows as disagreements ensue as to what kind of help and advice is needed. Neglect may be signalled to the statutory social services by concerned teachers or neighbours. The danger is that help might be angrily or passively rejected, resulting in the risk of self-imposed social exclusion, considered in more detail below.

Caring families

There are a large number of people who 'care' in many different formally organised situations, including foster care, residential care and hospital care. Nevertheless, 98% of children with disabilities live with their own families (Manthorpe, 1994). Most caring activity is carried out by related family members, who, as we have seen, usually refer to themselves not as carers but as parents, mothers, fathers, daughters and so on. A book on the experiences of bringing up a child with disabilities in the family is called

Positively Parents (Beresford, 1994), not *Positively Carers,* thus underlining the parent–child relationship rather than losing it in what is fast becoming the amorphous and ambiguous expression 'caring relationship'. The common concentration on parents rather than on children is often seen as 'natural' in the case of families where the child has a learning disability. Yet, despite the fact that parents are central in holding caring responsibilities for their child, their rights do not exceed the rights of the child, who must remain in focus.

Most research into caring for a child with a disability is about the carer and assumes that the main carer is the mother. Past surveys have directed questions at her alone (e.g. Ayer and Alaszewski, 1984; Glendinning, 1986; Smyth & Robus, 1989; McIntosh, 1992). The assumption is correct in most instances. In families where fathers help, a division of labour occurs, where mothers carry out child care tasks while fathers support by carrying out some household tasks. Cooke & Lawton's (1984) study found that mothers also did most household tasks, although they did find that men's participation in housework tended to increase with the severity of the child's disability.

Some more recent studies have attempted to focus on men as carers. Hornby's (1992) study of fathers' accounts of parenting children with disabilities suggests that they feel acutely the effects on family life and express anger and regret at what might have been. They are also less likely than mothers to have social support and contact with professionals. As the author points out, these accounts may not be representative because those interviewed were all middle-class and highly educated men. Social class differences in the general population in fathers' parenting and in a sense of identity as a father were reported by Smart & Neale (1999).

The evidence seems to support role and gender differences in the way mothers and fathers participate in, and perceive, caring for a child with a disability. This holds true whether the father is employed or not; and lower levels of employment have been reported among carers than in the general population (Green, 1985, 1988). Whatever their situation, fathers still see their role as providers: traditional breadwinners. Where there is disability in the family, this brings an added stress. A report by the National Children's Home (1994) found that the benefits system failed to compensate for the real costs of bringing up a child with disabilities. Lower levels of wages are also reported in such families (Baldwin, 1985; Editorial, 1993; Manthorpe, 1995), while financial need is higher because of extra costs (Baldwin, 1985; Smyth & Robus, 1989; Dobson & Middleton, 1998).

Smith & Brown (1989), in a feminist analysis of caring, conclude that caring work is ascribed low status and therefore continues to be regarded largely as women's work. The single parent as a lone carer is almost always the child's mother, mostly unable to work because of caring responsibilities and consequently suffering a large degree of isolation and other hardships (Roberts, 1988; Evandrou, 1990; Cigno with Burke, 1997).

All these studies concentrate on the carer first and the child second. This reflects the extra importance of parents for a child with learning disabilities; the methodological and ethical difficulties in communicating with children, particularly when they may have little or no speech and impaired intellectual functioning; and simply the 'double jeopardy' argument of the lack of power of children (and indeed adults) with disabilities. In most cases, although not all, the lot of the child is entwined with that of his or her carers; improvements in the quality of life for one family member will have an effect on the others'. Research reflects this fact. As we have said, keeping the child clearly in focus should enable the professional to avoid the provision of any services that might oppress the child. If the stresses and strains on carers are understood, services will enable them to continue with their day-to-day tasks. In this sense, the child's needs will also be met, since his or her well-being is closely aligned with that of the family.

CASE EXAMPLE: **Rebecca**

Rebecca is 13 and lives with her mother on a council estate in a remote village. Rebecca has a brother, Jonathan, aged 17, who lives with his father. The parents are divorced and parted before Rebecca's first birthday. Evidence of learning difficulties was not initially identified, although the mother felt something was wrong long before this was confirmed by the medical profession.

Behavioural difficulties now make Rebecca 'awkward to manage'. For example, in the past, according to her mother, she has broken dolls, 'just for the pleasure of breaking them'. Mother and child sleep in the same bedroom. Rebecca is a vulnerable child and 'easy prey' for anyone who takes interest in her.

Support was provided during Rebecca's early schooling where she received much individual attention from her class teacher. The teacher concerned is still in touch with the family, offering advice and other help. Her mother has many good friends who are her main source of support. Work is difficult to fit in with the various demands of looking after Rebecca. Sometimes Rebecca is taken out by her father at weekends, since the rift with her mother is now largely healed. There is little planning; the family 'takes each day as it comes'.

Comment

This case illustrates that a network of care exists for Rebecca's mother, in the form of informal support by friends and an ex-teacher. This mixing of personal and professional is not untypical of family support networks, such that the network does not square as formal or informal, but is a mixture of both. Perhaps this is a reflection of the underdevelopment of professional services, and so need is met in this way. It may just be the case that the informal is preferred to the formal and might therefore be considered an ideal solution. Rebecca's mother has her own personal life, with friends and acquaintances, without the need, it seems, for professional involvement. However, a holistic approach to family assessment, coordinated by a keyworker, might be acceptable to this family. A thorough assessment might identify new opportunities for Rebecca, for example.

Professional services could have a greater place in this family's life but choice needs to be real. No choice is not an option. A keyworker approach, which may take the form of three-monthly telephone calls in this case (a suggestion favoured by many parents), might make it more likely that at times of need help would be at hand. Rebecca and her mother would be more likely to express their views to someone who has served as a link and mediator over the years.

Conclusion

In our majority culture, the contemporary concept of the family is that of a nuclear unit that may or may not have extended family support. This reflects a relatively recent change which is due to improved health, welfare and social changes, such as increased mobility. Recently, child care legislation and accompanying guidance have paid more attention to the importance of relatives such as grandparents (Manthorpe, 1994).

The concept of dysfunctional and functional families can be used as a framework to describe the coping abilities of families. It is important to note that functional families may become dysfunctional at times during a lifetime of caring for a child with learning disabilities. Any family can change under stress; one consequence might be a retreat from community involvement, resulting in the exclusion of potential sources of social support and the risk of not meeting their child's needs.

We note that choice is the arbiter of whether services meet family needs or not, in order to avoid the sense of external control and lack of participation as citizens (see Chapter 9 on the locus of control). The family, its kinship and social networks need to be highly valued and supported by formal networks, which is the subject of the following chapter.

Chapter 5

Family Matters: Formal Support

The need to listen to and support carers is already evident from the explanatory material in Chapter 4, and is a consistent research finding (see Burke & Cigno, 1996). This is, of course, true for all of us. Being able to listen is a fundamental requirement for the qualification in social work (CCETSW, 1995). Implicit in this is the acknowledgement that, for many people, there are times when the routine sympathetic listening of relatives and friends is not sufficient or appropriate.

The discovery that a child has a learning disability has an immediate impact on the family, and may span a lifetime of care. One of the first reactions of parents is to ask each other: What happens now? How will we cope? and, Who can help? (see Chapters 2 and 3). In this chapter, we move from a consideration of how a family's informal networks offer support, or respond to parents' requests, to examine what help is on hand from formally organised helping sources, and whether this is automatically available or has to be sought.

In order to understand the mechanisms of support, we will identify the types of networks that are available to families as they undergo considerable emotional adjustments in coming to terms with the fact that their child is different. Professional involvement should be directly concerned with people's experiences, providing support linked to the reality of views expressed by those people with first-hand knowledge of what it is like to encounter disability. Later, the same people will be able to give professionals feedback on the quality and quantity of services received (Cigno, 1995a).

In this chapter, the concept of networks and their relationship with organised care in the community is introduced. We explore why some families cope either alone or with limited community support services. Is this a matter of choice or are they left alone because of a lack of social networks and scarce resources? A basic characteristic of support services should be that they are set up in such a way that vulnerable individuals are not left to cope alone, unless it is their expressed wish and there are no issues of risk to a child's care and development.

Community care

The former junior health minister, Paul Boateng, promised that the government would listen to carers before developing new strategies. He recognised, too, that there are different kinds of caring, but that they all have certain needs in common:

> 'What knits these disparate groups together is their need for *information* ... The government does recognise that caring can be a difficult task, often undertaken at great personal cost. But ... carers do not need fine words from me. What is wanted most is *practical help* and *support,* and proper *respite* from the tasks of [caring] ...' (our italics)

> (Boateng, 1998).

Ironically, this article (Boateng, 1998, in *Community Care*) was soon followed by another in the same journal, where it was argued that carer support was 'still a neglected area' (Henwood, 1998). The White Paper (Department of Health, 1999) to which Boateng referred is now published, but it is too early to judge what its impact may be. More recently, evidence has come to light that there is less recognition and support for ethnic minority families caring for a disabled child. Although their level of need is higher compared with white families, they experience more difficulty in accessing services, are more socially isolated and are less satisfied with services they do receive (Chambra *et al.*, 1999).

The current experience of any isolated, distressed family unit where there is an individual with learning disabilities is out of keeping with the spirit of care in the community. Barnes (1997) notes that:

> 'The objective of community care should be to enable those previously excluded from the community to participate within it'

> (p. 155).

The principle of care in the community is, seemingly, to assist the more needy families, or individuals, by providing a failsafe network of care which both supports and sustains them. In the Barclay Report (1982), which precedes this sense of care *by* the community, social workers were expected to become involved in 'social care planning' (p. 33), the sense being that of caring *for* the community. The Griffiths Report (Griffiths, 1988) and the subsequent National Health Service and Community Care Act 1990 both emphasised the importance of community care, guided by professionals, to ensure that individual and family needs are met, and that services follow needs rather than the converse. Activating support networks should therefore become the task of the professional, in particular the social worker, who can identify which families or individuals experience some element of social exclusion Burke (1997a). Assessments should be based on the family's expressed needs, mediated by informed professional opinion. Middleton (1998) expresses this well when she suggests that social workers' views of need should be triangulated with those of parents.

Practitioners are required to work in partnership with those in other agencies, with the client (or service user, an increasingly preferred term) *and* the carer, a policy also underlined in the Children Act 1989 and the subsequent *Working Together* guidance (Department of Health, 1991; Department of Health, Home Office, Department for Education and Employment, 1999). The use of respite care, to which we refer elsewhere, particularly in Chapter 11, illustrates the point: it serves the needs of client and carer but very often more specifically the latter because of the common need for a break from caring in order to carry on serving the needs of the cared-for. The Carers National Association came into being to highlight such needs as well as the perceived lack of support from community services for carers, who may be 'pushed to the limits of endurance' (Pitkeathley, 1995). There has been a suggestion that offering training to carers offers some recognition of the fact that they 'save the public purse millions of pounds' (Rowe & Goodman, 1995).

Not all families need or want the kind of help they perceive professionals can provide. One concept of care in the community is reflected by the experience of families who, although in the community, are self-supportive rather than users of helping networks. Care in the community is all too often not care by the community. Community is a mere location, not a supportive structure for living.

Caring for a disabled child can be made more difficult for the carers because professionals and service providers often lack sufficient understanding of the child's disability and the family's needs, a recurring theme in our work. In such cases, parents may find that self-help is the only way to get their child's needs met. After all, they have first-hand knowledge of their child, so rightly expect professionals to be knowledgeable, listen to their views and spend time getting to know their child. Following the NHS and Community Care Act 1990, local authority procedures made clear that the user's views on his or her needs must be recorded together with the practitioner's (usually a social worker's) assessment. A note should be made of the shortfall, if any, between these assessments and what can actually be provided. However, the carer's views, which may be different, even contrasting, must also be noted, and if the carer has identified needs of his or her own, then there comes a point when he or she is also a client and a service user in his or her own right. Formal recognition of this principle is contained in the Carers (Recognition and Services) Act 1995.

Professional responsibilities

The role of the social work professional as a coordinator of support and advice is crucial to the well-being of such families, for whom the matching of available services requires an understanding of their expressed needs. Some rationing of services is inevitable but families need to have a real sense of choice and of control. Although the role of coordinator usually falls to the social worker, all practitioners need to take care to communicate among themselves: this is what families want and expect and is now close to mandatory, as the effects of the government's White Paper (Department of Health, 1998) become visible in practice.

Different professionals hold differing responsibilities concerning community care. Lockyer & Gilbert (1995) observe that social workers and nurses in the area of learning disabilities approach their task in different ways. Despite this, their levels and kinds of intervention may develop similarly, overlap or become more specialised. Recent research on a multi-agency family approach to the needs of children with disabilities demonstrates that professionals have to work hard to achieve what families want: a seamless, holistic service (Cigno & Gore, 1998; see Chapter 10).

Community nurses, for example, deal with behavioural problems while social workers, who may or should have a similar expertise, are often more concerned, not least in parents' minds, with child protection issues. We have found that social workers rarely see behavioural problems as part of their remit, or indeed feel qualified to intervene in this significant area of work (see Chapter 11). However, blurred boundaries do exist among professionals in the delivery of services and in providing social support. Professionals can also assist each other in explaining their respective roles, in offering mutual support and ensuring that this clarity is conveyed to the families concerned.

CASE EXAMPLE: **Michael**

Michael, aged nine years, is the youngest of three children. His older brothers are 13 and 15. The family live in a specially adapted semi-detached house.

A range of specialists has been involved with dietary needs, aids for the home and medical matters. According to the parents, the general practitioner (GP) is interested only when Michael is 'poorly', otherwise the family 'get on with it'. Holiday play schemes are helpful during the summer. Michael unfortunately has been intellectually outgrown by his peers. His mental age has been estimated to be about four years compared with his chronological age of nine. His brothers are very protective and object if they feel his parents are 'telling him off', because Michael 'can't help it'. For example, he once put bubble bath and an excess of toilet tissues down the toilet to the exasperation of his parents, accompanied by a spirited defence by his brothers.

Michael's parents find support from friends who provide a listening ear, but they do not use the extended family, who can only manage if the children are in bed. Only then do they feel able to act as passive babysitters, with the telephone at hand if some emergency develops. The parents found parent groups 'too confrontational', focused on arguments about how difficult one child is compared with another and lacking recognition that each child is different. Michael 'does not have fits like some children' but he is able, for example, to lean over a fireguard to operate a gas fire, thereby presenting a danger to himself and to others.

Both parents feel that they have had to fight for every service requested. Each professional person, they say, operates in isolation, whereas there is a need for one professional to have a detailed grasp of family needs. Michael is a well-known local figure so he tends to be treated as rather special, which his parents feel is not always helpful to their attempts to set limits and 'normalise' his behaviour.

Comment

Michael's family are self-supportive despite some internal family differences about how he should be treated. Professional help is seemingly uncoordinated with no sense of partnership with the family. Families new to the experience of having a child with profound learning difficulties do not always know how best to act in their child's interest due to the initial distress and emotional conflicts of having a disabled child. As matters stand, parents are forced into decisions they are not clear about, whereas they need help to appreciate fully the consequences of their actions. Professionals are in danger of being too glib or dismissive about such needs. They require training to understand that, even when a family is not dysfunctional, the stresses that exist could push them over the edge, making regular and supportive monitoring of the family's needs a necessity for their well-being. Michael's needs should not be considered in isolation from those of his siblings, who would also benefit from some support (see Chapter 6).

Promoting care

We use the word 'care' to denote the task carried out by parents who care for their child with learning disabilities. The word carer may denote an informal relationship with the cared-for (Twigg & Atkin, 1995). It is also increasingly used to describe the formal relationship between paid employee and service user. Home helps are now usually called community carers and residential staff are known as care workers or just carers. These changes in meanings appear to come about because of the need to label worker–client relationships as caring, perhaps in the hope that by using the word 'care' in a job title, the employee will live up to it. In fact, some social services departments have changed their title to 'social care'. It has become convenient to use one term to describe any formal or informal relationship between any person of any age who has dependency needs and the person of any age and relationship who attempts to meet that need. One result may be a devaluing of the concept of caring by overuse of the word.

Individual care usually relates to the carer's role, which involves looking after someone. We tend to think of individual or personal care as helping, supporting and protecting other people (Finklestein, 1993). How help and support are provided is an issue in terms of whose responsibility it is: individual, group, personal or professional? Reflection and analysis can help clarify role and tasks and lead to useful planning strategies.

The idea of care incorporates such values as the need to ameliorate distress and improve client autonomy and quality of life (Finklestein, 1993). It does not mean taking over a person's life by controlling experiences for that individual and denying choice, whether this is, say, choice of food, companionship or the wish for one's own space. Exclusion from social events and relationships is a restriction most would not accept for themselves, yet it occurs in the case of many cared-for persons. Explanations are sometimes used to cover up action: 'He doesn't like being with people,' 'It's far too noisy for her,' ' She's not hungry.' Such forms of restrictions may imply the opposite values to care, even though well intentioned. In fact, many people, including professionals, often direct their questions to the carer, as the BBC radio programme entitled *Does He Take Sugar?* famously highlighted. The message given is muddled, revealing both an attitude of protection towards, and the weakness of, the care giver's authority over another person.

Organising care on behalf of another can, on the other hand, be helpful in encouraging a move from dependency to independency. Control in such an example may involve planning work and facilitating tasks by a keyworker. The power relationship in hospitals where barriers exist between staff and patients, due to the dependency of patients on staff and the variable nature of the relationship, works against empowering individuals to make choices for themselves. Values underpinning this form of control may more usually include concepts of prevention, exclusion, elimination or manipulation of what is a perceived natural right (Finklestein, 1993). The justification for such a regime in organisations or actions in the personal sphere is the incapacity of the other to make choices; an underlying value might be the maintenance of an easier life for the institution or the home (see Chapter 9).

The notion of choice arises in all spheres of a child's life. We have seen how important this is in selecting the right form of education, and noted that families are largely satisfied with schools and teachers where they were involved in choosing from alternatives. This issue is also discussed in reflections on special and inclusive education in other countries (see, for example, Porter & Kelly, 1998). Inequalities in exercising choice, such as being able to go to the lavatory, have a shower or go to a film when you want to, have also been explored in research by the National Children's Home (1994).

A key theme that networks demonstrate when effectively operational and one which pervades the concept of care in the community is the distribution of power and equality. There is a need to compare and contrast professional power with the needs of the user and the imperative to work together to achieve agreed goals. The empowerment of carers is promoted by establishing, or helping to establish, effective social networks which then assist in overcoming inequality, even despair, induced by a sense of learned helplessness in carers and users alike (Seligman, 1975).

From the above, it is clear that care and control can represent opposing value systems. Support is generally associated with a positive caring function while exclusion, more often, has negative connotations since it denies the choice of becoming involved. However, care may well also include elements of restriction, especially when it is aimed at preventing harm. Apparently, then, care and protection can indicate both differing and similar values depending on whether choices are made freely or are denied due to lack of agreement or indecision regarding what constitutes an acceptable level of risk in the home. The carer is often the person who both makes opportunities available and places restrictions on the cared-for. The social context may amplify this dilemma in the community where choice has within it an inherent element of risk-taking.

A sense of community can be fostered over a large geographical area through an identification with the functional activities of an organisation. This is quite unlike the traditional neighbourhood community network as portrayed by Young & Willmott (1957) in their Bethnal Green study, where residents lived entwined lives in close proximity. It moves us on to think of families who use a particular and specialist form of care not necessarily available within the smaller familial type of neighbourhood network. We call this phenomenon a community of interest.

Social networks

Networks, for our purposes, can include both the informal relationships of kin and friendship and formal relationships, as might exist at work or in any number of professional or advisory contacts. Such relationships may be face-to-face or sustained through other means such as letters, the telephone and, increasingly, the Internet.

The concept of a social network helps us to evaluate care needs within the context of a local community by determining (1) whether they exist at a formal or informal level, (2) how useful any existing networks are for the people concerned, and (3) whether networks need augmenting by professional involvement from health, welfare or educational services (Burke & Cigno, 1997).

Evaluating the effectiveness of social networks needs to begin with identifying the type of network: either informal, for example, good neighbourhood schemes or kinship networks; (see Pereira, 1989; Snaith, 1989), or formal, where the role of the professional is to help establish or reinforce existing supportive networks (see Bulmer, 1985). Networks do not have to be geographically restricting. Many voluntary organisations have both a national and a local network, where the national focus is on policy, government lobbying and highlighting the needs of particular groups, and the local focus is on bringing together individuals in a similar situation or condition as well as home visiting. An example of an organisation defined by age is Age Concern and one defined by condition is SCOPE, the charity for people with cerebral palsy. Martin House Children's Hospice (Burke, 1991) covers a wide geographical area – the north of England and Scotland – but also provides paid workers who contact families locally with the purpose of providing emotional support and counselling, backed up with the opportunity for respite care for the whole family should stresses and strains become too burdensome.

The notion of a formal network helps us to identify a further theme that pervades the concept of care in the community: partnership. This is manifest in the work of professionals, like the Martin House contact workers, who help facilitate the development of supportive networks. Professional responsibilities should include partnership with the carer as well as with the child concerned. The aim of working in partnership is to achieve agreed solutions in order to meet the needs of users, in this case children with learning disabilities. It is our view that carers are empowered to meet these needs only when effective and supportive social networks valued by users and their families are in place. Networks that facilitate social contacts do much to help overcome the sense of inequality and helplessness that often occurs when dealing with formal, especially statutory, services. This position typifies the situation of the more socially isolated carers for whom professional solutions seem the only ones possible.

Changing networks: analytical techniques

The dynamic quality of networks can be harnessed to overcome problems arising when individuals seek some form of support. First, networks change spontaneously over time: an examination that does not take this into account may not reflect this varying quality. People are not necessarily set rigidly in certain networks. A representation of a network often therefore reflects a snapshot of experience at a particular time. An important factor in children's needs at any one time is their age and level of development. Understanding networks requires the capacity to capture the sense of the dynamic: the change and fluidity of life experiences. Second, networks interact, and a focus on one individual or family will necessarily include others who in turn have their own networks. Third, networks can be helped to change and develop. This last point is especially relevant to families experiencing the impact of learning disability and their relationship with professional helpers. This understanding can then illuminate the experience of others at times of stress and difficulty.

A useful understanding of social networks is provided by Atkinson & Williams (1990), who identify six headings that can be used as a basis for undertaking any network analysis. These are: *locality, reciprocity, isolation, stress, friendships* and *attachment*. Each heading is used to consider the nature of a particular network. For example, developing support based on *locality* can mean that it is necessary to establish neighbourhood schemes to help parents and children with learning disabilities share common problems through local 'access points' available to them. *Reciprocity* is about giving and taking; offering support has a pay-off and can be rewarding for all parties. Usually a family, particularly if isolated, is able to cope much better if someone shows interest or is supportive. The achievement of reciprocity means that support is mutual and non-stigmatising, with a clear potential to relieve stress and prevent breakdown. Some parents, though, as we have said, might appear not to want a social network, but the choice needs to be theirs as an entitlement, not a privilege.

Friendships can develop between formal carer and client, as well as in the more traditional, informal sense, as between a teaching aide and child. Friendship is basic to the human condition and, without friendship, caring can too easily become a wearisome, routinised task, lacking warmth. *Attachment* is more than a consequence of friendship, it is about a basic commitment rooted in the caring we both feel for others and need from them. Social networks are composed of such elements; examining a network will accordingly provide an understanding of the complexities of life from a variety of perspectives.

Atkinson & Williams (1990) also consider network populations, size and shape of networks, formal or informal structures, links among individuals, and the direction of contacts (i.e. their reciprocal nature). Atkinson (1989) describes the quantitative processes that are required when studying the nature of social networks involving people with learning difficulties. This involves an understanding of who makes contact with whom, the strength of the bond which develops, whether communication is two-way or unidirectional and indeed the number of contacts that are made within any network, thus forming a linking social structure among any number of individuals.

Atkinson largely excludes the qualitative element of individually expressed needs which form the hub of this book. A quantitative analysis provides a knowledge base (see Henwood's (1998) review of statistics concerning carers; and a survey of provision for special needs children in Wales reported by Jones & Ware (1997)), which enables those with power and authority to bring about change, usually in the form of targeted resources. Without parallel human understanding of people's lives, the voice of the relatively powerless user is too often mute (Hubert, 1991). Ascertaining who is central to the analysis is the first important step.

Effective networks and services

An effective network means that the system is both supportive and helpful to the user. A network may exist as emergency response services – for example, health, police and fire services – and in such cases support becomes secondary to the more basic need for individual survival and protection. However, while support is secondary when life itself is threatened, it remains, in most cases, vitally important for promoting an individual's well-being. Social networks, for most people, are an essential source of support. This is qualified when the individual who is helped considers that a relationship of sufficient significance is formed, within which a positive contribution to their situation can be made. In other words, the offer of support is perceived as helpful by the recipient. Supportive relationships are based on mutual involvement requiring trust and a shared understanding of concerns to be faced.

Effective services should not be confused with efficient services; the former meets needs, the latter may be more concerned with smooth operation and cost but may not necessarily meet needs. This distinction has been clarified, though not to the satisfaction of all, in the many commentaries accompanying the government's 'Best Value' policy (for example, Donovan, 1999; Fletcher, 1999). If a request for help receives a prompt response, then it suggests efficiency, but this does not mean that the service provided is 'quality' or effective. Therefore, the client or user may be initially satisfied by the speed but later dissatisfied because the service is not perceived as useful. The difference is important. There is also a question of who determines need: the carer and user should have a say in which services are provided (for a discussion of needs-led assessments, see the White Paper *Caring for People* (Department of Health, 1989, paragraph 2.5).

Essentially, effectiveness is to do with perceived benefits to user and carer as well as meaningful improvements to the quality and perhaps quantity of care. A sense of inequality exists when professionals take away the right of the user to participate in decisions about service requirements, or respond to the carer at the expense of the user. When cost is a major issue in providing services, this should be made clear by the professional involved. The reason for the decision not to provide a service must be written down and shared with the family; any shortfall between a recognised need for a service and its actual provision must be recorded.

If services are not valued, then they are not perceived as effective; and if a network of support is not of a form that the user requires, then this, too, is likely to be ineffective. Nevertheless, service providers in the public domain have a duty to pursue efficiency since resources will always be rationed, but clearly this should not be at the cost of ignoring needs and evaluating effectiveness.

Social exclusion

Examining the need for professional support, Byrne *et al.* (1988) reported that families with well-developed informal networks need less help. This might explain why professionals target families where there are few identifiable sources of support. On the other hand, we also found that assertive, middle-class parents with well-developed social skills were adept at attracting resources:

> 'It seems that unless one's pushy, one doesn't get services – but I've had a good service'

> (mother of eight-year-old Katy, in Burke & Cigno, 1996, p. 87).

The question of access to benefits and allowances is a case in point. These fluctuate, not only making it difficult for carers and practitioners to keep up to date, but also to help families work out their entitlement. However, most local authorities have for some years employed benefits officers or advisers, independent of the government Benefits Agency, able to work this out, checking that the child and carer are receiving the correct amount and type of allowance or benefit. Disability Alliance also offer this service, much needed because, unhappily, the Department of Social Security staff have been known to make errors. Many families in our survey (Burke & Cigno, 1996) would have been helped by such a service, since parents told us that they had found out about 'what you're entitled to' by chance, often through other parents.

Although we did not study which financial benefits were taken up, our interview data indicated that the most socially and financially disadvantaged families were most likely to underclaim: not pushy enough, as Katy's mother implied. A systematic recent study of 18 000 disabled children confirms this: a large number of such families failed to claim the Disability Living Allowance, although their child clearly met the criteria (Roberts & Lawton, 1999).

Isolation may compound the strain and anger involved in caring, particularly when professionals, who have a responsibility to reach out to families, do not fully clarify in their own minds the goals of their work. Our research (Burke & Cigno, 1996; Burke, 1997a and b) identified the need for family support precisely to prevent social exclusion in practice. Social workers, through their education and training, might be expected to be at the forefront of organising support networks. Where they lack the skills to do this, they need further training to develop confidence in this area. They also require assessment and advocacy skills to identify what children and families need and the ability to convey this to service purchasers and providers.

Having considered the basic differences between formal and informal networks and the nature of social exclusion, we turn to a case example to illustrate the difficulties of care in the community where there is also an enforced lack of social and familial networks. This family has been featured before (see Burke & Cigno, 1996) but is included again here in an updated form, after follow-up research by Burke (1997). This later study confirmed that isolation continues to exist for some families and that the offer of adequate service provision is still fraught with difficulties through the age span of childhood and adolescence.

CASE EXAMPLE: **Sarah**

Sarah, 12 years old, lives with her mother in a terraced house. The ground floor has a special bedroom adaptation, paid for by her mother with assistance from a Disabled Facilities Grant administered by the local authority. Sarah and her mother have lived together since her mother separated from Sarah's father. Her father has custody of Sarah's older brother, James.

Sarah has a neuro-degenerative disease: sufferers rarely survive their late teens. Currently, she is confined to a wheelchair and is totally dependent on carers. She has moderate to severe learning disabilities.

Numerous health, education and social services representatives are in contact with the family and all offer some support, according to each organisation's responsibilities. The net experience, however, has not been good because low-level professional understanding seems to characterise most contacts. Practitioners' assessments of need either differ from the mother's or acknowledge the service need while noting that the service is not available. Advice regarding Sarah's bedroom adaptation was so slow in coming that Sarah's mother was at the point of giving up waiting and was about to seek private means for providing for her daughter's needs.

Sarah's mother feels anger and frustration towards all agencies. No family support is available locally and friends are few. Mother and child are isolated, particularly at weekends and during holiday periods when the mother provides one-to-one care for her daughter. Mobility is a problem, because Sarah needs special transportation equipment to enable her wheelchair to fit into a vehicle; help with funding is still awaited from the motability charity. The sad postscript to Sarah's case is that she died before this became available.

Comment

This case illustrates the difficulty with care in the community because of the state of isolation of mother and child due to the mother's circumstances and the care regime which Sarah required. However, it might still be described as care in the community, since care was provided, but was not perceived by Sarah's mother as supportive. Relationships with service sector carers were difficult due to poor past experiences, so Sarah's mother largely got by on her own.

Professionals clearly need to make allowance for the plight of such isolated families. Rather than entering into a series of stress-inducing communications, confrontations even, involving the inability to provide resources due to their scarcity, practitioners need actively to identify other support services which might assist with the mother's caring task while acknowledging her right to be angry over refusals and delays. Sarah's mother probably would have benefited from counselling to help her to adjust to the situation her daughter faced, plus some weekend relief care to enable her to find some time for herself, thereby better managing her routine and recovering her strength to give more quality time to Sarah. The professional has to be seen to be part of the support available to the carer, not an intrusion, otherwise the carer's task is made more stressful. The risk to all is that service provision decreases at a time when it is most urgently needed. Working relationships need building; in order to do this, basic practical help needs to be available quickly. Daly (1998) comments on what has already been only too well documented over the last two decades: lack of agency coordination and families' struggles for services.

Conclusion

In this chapter we introduced the framework of support which we call social networks. We show that contacts exist at all levels, from states of near isolation, with little help, to the more socially and professionally involved families who receive help which might, nevertheless, not meet all their needs. We have shown that networks exist in all spheres of life, from telephone contacts to meeting people within one's neighbourhood. Support is experienced when contacts offer some form of desired help. This is often on the basis of a mutual understanding, a reciprocal relationship, more evident in informal support situations. We examined the idea that people may live in isolated states, but that this might not be a matter of their personal choice. The need is to make choices available to people who previously may not have had a say over their lives, or who have developed a poor view of service provision. This is a concept fundamental to care in the community: if an option is not offered, then a choice cannot be made either to accept or to refuse.

There is admittedly a subjective element in a family's assessment of its own situation and of where its members find or need support. A 'good practice' assessment should enhance existing support, modifying a subjective assessment if necessary with the full understanding and cooperation of those involved. Professional services should attempt to meet individual needs, rather than impose a limited range of services which, though efficient, might be ineffective in meeting needs. All too often provision does not meet assessed needs. It should be remembered that contact, although important, is not necessarily the same as support; it could be insignificant, intrusive, unhelpful or even dangerous, particularly if the advice offered is likely to result in mistakes or wrongful decisions being reached. Professional involvement should include the full participation of children, as far as possible, and their parents. A thorough assessment of the help that the situation requires will also need the involvement of all agencies potentially of use to the family. A detailed example of how a multi-agency approach can achieve this is the subject of Chapter 10.

Chapter 6

Brothers and Sisters

In this chapter, we explore the issues for brothers and sisters who may experience displacement, disruption or disturbance in family life; and suggest an approach aimed at helping to reaffirm the standing of siblings in the family. It should be remembered that the attachment between one sibling and another is the longest most individuals have (McHale & Gamble, 1987). Demonstrating an understanding of the needs of siblings helps them to manage at home and at school, and has an influence on their future lifespan of experience with their disabled brother or sister.

A self-evident point repeated throughout the literature (McCormack, 1978; Glendinning, 1986) is that children with learning disabilities require more help and support from carers than other children. Such attention has the likely consequence of allowing less time for brothers and sisters in the family, a point less often made until relatively recently. According to Atkinson & Crawforth (1995), drawing on figures for 1989, 80% of children with disabilities have non-disabled siblings; we are therefore talking about a phenomenon affecting the vast majority of families where there is a disabled child.

While we believe that it is true that the presence of a disabled child may bring new opportunities and understanding to other family members, we also feel that it may mean that the needs of brothers and sisters receive less attention. Such differences are found to some degree in any family but risks may be greater in families with a disabled child, especially when the child concerned has difficulty in expressing their needs, or cannot express matters as clearly as their siblings, relatives or friends. The focus here is therefore on the particular needs of siblings, who have different experiences from those of children without a disabled brother or sister. Siblings also require some attention if professionals are to help the whole family. The Department of Health (1991), in its *Guidance and Regulations,* clearly recognises this need, stating that siblings' needs 'should be provided for as part of a package of services for the child with a disability' (section 6.4, p. 13).

In order to understand the situation of brothers and sisters, it is useful to distinguish between the special needs of a child with learning disabilities and those of a brother or sister. We shall illustrate how these differences affect their lives and draw on the evidence available from case examples to show how professional attention and assessment might identify brothers' and sisters' needs and point to ways in which they might be met (Burke & Montgomery, 2000).

We start by assessing the difference that having a learning disabled sibling makes to brothers and sisters.

The needs of siblings

The birth of a child will have an impact on the lives of siblings, for the new baby will make demands which have to be met above all by his or her carers. At the very least, this is an extra focus of interest but, with a new baby in the family, it is also a source of potential stress, because the family is experiencing the effects of a major change to its constitution. A child with learning disabilities will not only be different in various ways, but will certainly require even more attention from carers (Moeller, 1986), either from birth, or following the identification of disability. The level of attention is likely to continue, and may increase where the disabilities are severe, for as long as the child remains at home.

As we found in our research, talking about carers means talking about parents. Consequences of family caring are that these additional demands leave less time and opportunity for parental attention to be given to other children. Brothers and sisters of disabled children, as Glendinning (1986) notes, 'may experience handicaps and disadvantages as well' (p. 3). This can be a result of being 'left out', adding further to the differences perceived by siblings. Parents are often only too well aware that siblings may suffer from a lack of attention: 48% of parents, according to an Offfice of Population Censuses and Surveys (OPCS) survey (Bone & Meltzer, 1989), were aware that they had less time for other siblings. Where one child had several disabilities, 72% of parents thought that siblings were affected in some way (Department of Health and Social Welfare, 1986). A few years earlier, Butler *et al.* (1978) found that, according to their mothers, many siblings had their homework, property and friendships disrupted by a child with severe learning disabilities in the family.

Sibling rivalry is nothing new, but in the context of an additional burden to parents that coping with a child with learning disabilities brings, then sibling reactions may include adverse emotional stress (Seligman & Darling, 1989), which they share, according to their age, to some degree with their parents at the time of the birth or realisation of the presence of disability (Seligman, 1991). This often goes unrecognised. This kind of family refocusing which results from the presence of the newborn infant can lead to resentment by siblings who feel that their brother or sister requires and gains too much attention and disproportionate consideration (Coleman, 1990).

Like parents, brothers and sisters need information about disability, a need that will change over time with their understanding and according to the differences in the developmental stages achieved by the disabled child in the family. Pre-school children, for instance, need simple 'concrete' explanations suitable for their developmental level (Lobato, 1990). Kew (1975) found that parents' ability to cope with a disabled child was one of the factors affecting the welfare of siblings. A readjustment to the new situation is necessary, balancing the competing demands which, as Powell & Ogle (1985) recognise, affect both the structure of the newly constituted family and its functional ability to manage.

It is important, therefore, to understand how siblings cope with the change in their status and standing compared with children in non-disabled families, and whether the consequences of any additional burdens placed upon them are redressed in other ways. While, as we said earlier, most parents believe that their children might be affected by a learning-disabled sibling, this does not necessarily mean in an adverse way, since learning-disabled children bring their own rewards.

Watson (1991) gives an example of one grown-up sister who talks of her 'sense of responsibility', leading her to 'inform others about the realities of Down syndrome', even agreeing to speak to groups about this (p. 108). In earlier work, Lobato *et al.* (1987) and Blackard & Barsch (1982) showed that relationships within families were strengthened when caring for a child with disabilities, a finding which somewhat conflicts with others mentioned elsewhere. Frude (1991) discusses these differences, suggesting that, while some families experience caring for a disabled child as a crisis, others become more united, working together to overcome difficulties.

Siblings of children with disabilities develop special qualities, and while all children have the capacity to respond to and care for others, the way in which they do so reflects their own individual differences. These need time to be understood, for the vulnerability of childhood is such that misunderstanding may provoke a lifetime of uncertainty. Weighing up the available evidence, we conclude that in most cases the daily challenges will be perceived as greater by parents; and siblings are in danger of not always having normal childhood expectations met. As they grow up and ponder their future role, brothers and sisters, unlike the young woman quoted above by Watson, may increasingly feel that they face many of the challenges experienced by their parents (Mayer & Vadasy, 1997).

Twelve-year-old Kelsey's case, which emerged from a research interview focusing on family support, is one illustration of this process.

CASE EXAMPLE: Kelsey and David

Kelsey had in the past asked few questions about her brother David, aged ten, who was born with cerebral palsy. He was intellectually impaired, had little speech and walked with difficulty.

Until a few years ago, the two had played together. Realising that David's reading and concentration were poor, Kelsey had made him little picture books 'to teach him to read'. She had been struck by how her friends stared at David when they came to the house. One little girl had refused to go into the paddling pool on one hot summer's day because 'your brother's been in there'. Kelsey had been anxious about such incidents, but had not spoken about them before. Neither had her parents.

One day 'out of the blue' she said thoughtfully to her mother, 'I suppose I shall have to look after David one day when you and Daddy can't.' Her mother was completely taken aback. She tried to reassure her daughter that this was not the case. She felt proud of her daughter's sense of responsibility at such a young age, while at the same time was upset and at a loss at this evidence of the impact of David's needs on his sister and on her thoughts about her own and his future.

Comment: the role for the practitioner

Neither Kelsey nor her mother were prepared for feelings about growing up with a learning and physically disabled child in the family. Kelsey had come to realise that her brother could rarely share in joint activities any more. She carried guilt about the divergence of their lives; her observations of her parents' lives had led her to the conclusion that, one day, this would be her life too. Her mother did not know how to help her, only rushing to reassure her that she did not have to carry the burden of responsibility for David. Both mother and daughter need someone to whom they can talk about their situation. Gardner & Smyly (1997) indicate that because situations and relationships change over time, support should continue to be available whenever it is needed. A sibling support group would probably benefit Kelsey at this stage, alleviating her sense of isolation while enabling her to share her feelings with other children with similar experiences.

Zatlow (1992) gives an example of a sister's guilt after she had left home. She still felt the need to be near her family in order to return to help with her disabled brother; and often did so, to her mother's relief. Such young women may also fear that they might give birth to a disabled child, underlining the need for support and information across the lifespan. This may include the availability of genetic counselling. Barr (1999) suggests that a non-disabled sibling will need counselling in order to share their anxieties and concerns. Powell & Ogle (1985) also stress that parents need to talk to their children about future plans for their disabled child. They may require help to do so. With some resolution or acceptance of the child's disability will come a greater sense of making time for their non-disabled child. Professional alertness to these needs should be part of a practitioner's repertoire of helping knowledge and skills.

Parental and sibling stress

The way parents adjust to the discovery that their child has a learning disability will significantly affect stresses to family life (Chetwynd, 1985; Cairns, 1992; Burke & Cigno, 1996). Such stresses bring further consequences. There is evidence that families under stress have difficulty in managing day-to-day matters and risk breakdown if even minor crises cannot be resolved (Frude, 1991; Beresford, 1994). Family disruption is worse for families experiencing additional problems, such as financial worries, not necessarily associated with bringing up a child with disabilities. This may have further repercussions on the children concerned (Gath, 1974). Siblings may be expected to compensate for their brother or sister not only by helping at home to relieve the parental burden of care but also through pressure to achieve academically, or in sporting activities, points also made by Coleman (1990).

Coping with school

A lone mother in our 1995 survey (see also Cigno with Burke, 1997) described how her husband had left the family home during their developmentally delayed daughter's first year at school:

> 'He buried his head in the sand and I got little support. [Daughter] was affected and her younger brother had to have counselling'
>
> (Burke & Cigno, 1996, p. 74).

In another instance, a lone mother told us with some bitterness that the family had broken down due to stress (see Chapter 7); she had kept the child with learning disabilities and her husband the 'normal' child. Yet another family, this time still intact with both parents, presented the view that when Simon (the disabled child) was at home, everything centred around him and what he was able to take part in. His two brothers had to take a back seat.

School-aged siblings may themselves develop behavioural problems, indicating the need for teacher awareness and training. Jenkinson (1998) found that negative attitudes at school tended to stereotype siblings as different from their peers, and identified the fault as a lack of training given to teachers. Siblings face difficulties at school, find it difficult to bring friends home and suffer loss of self-esteem (Dyson, 1996). The association with a disabled brother or sister can be stigmatising (Frude, 1991), making it difficult for them to form attachments with other children at school. This partly reflects the reality that many children have never come across disability at close quarters and do not know how to cope with it. Children also, of course, reflect their parents' attitudes to disabled people.

The following case shows that, even at the age of seven, a child may experience difficulties at school, marking her out as different from her school peers.

CASE EXAMPLE: Fay and Paul

Paul is five and a half years old. He has an older sister, Fay, who is seven. The family live in a large, terraced house in a market town. At the age of 18 months, Paul was diagnosed as having learning disabilities. His condition is similar to the 'clumsy child' syndrome, dyspraxia. This affects the motor neurological pathways. He seems not to notice pain. Paul has attended special school from the age of four.

Respite care and holiday provision for Paul are helpful to the family. For example, he attends the summer play scheme, allowing more family time for Fay. She experiences difficulty at school, becoming upset by comments from other children like 'your brother's stupid'. Paul loves his sister and they play happily together at home. However, maintaining school friendships has proven difficult for Fay, possibly because she does her best to stand by her brother and does not tolerate jibes about him. Unfortunately, her protective instincts towards him seem to promote more rather than less intolerant behaviour from other schoolchildren. Her parents feel that she will need special qualities to help her through school; she is being forced to mature and grow up beyond her years.

Comment

This case example gives the impression of a well-adjusted family doing their best to manage, but despite this, Fay is suffering because of the attitude of other children in her school. Fay needs support, while the attitude, or at least the behaviour, of her peers needs changing. This might well require some action to be taken by Fay's teachers, who clearly need to do something to address the unacceptable behaviour of those children who taunt. Bullying is now taken seriously in most schools, following dramatic cases of children who have suffered in this way (La Fontaine, 1991; Miles, 1994). There is, moreover, some recent evidence that children with learning and other disabilities are regularly bullied at school (La Fontaine, 1991); in such situations, where brothers and sisters attend the same school, they want to come to the rescue, as a brother in Morrow's (1992) study explains:

> 'I'm used to being kind to my brother and sister . . . But, if someone starts a fight, I will fight. I won't put up with anyone teasing Wade or Jolene'

(p. 4).

Fay, too, needs an opportunity to discuss her difficulties, for she could in time come to resent her brother for her situation. Standing up for Paul has led to further taunts of increased intensity and frequency. Some therapeutic input, as well as a firm anti-bullying policy in school, would help teachers and the children concerned to deal with confrontations, but this kind of intervention is not easily available and might not be spontaneously sought either by children who are bullied or by their parents. A peer support group may help, providing Fay can be convinced that such a group would be helpful to her and that such provision is at hand (see Chapter 10).

Parental views

We have commented above and elsewhere (Burke & Cigno, 1995) on the polarisation of family views concerning the impact of a brother or sister with learning disabilities on siblings. Essentially, the positive view is reflected by one mother, who commented:

> 'They all get on very well. They love each other.'

The opposite view is offered by another parent:

> 'They don't get on well. Richard tends to smack, he gets excited . . . he smacks because he can't communicate.'

The reality for most families is likely to be somewhere in between these two contrasting views. In our 1995 research, the relationship among most siblings appeared somewhat ambivalent (Burke & Cigno, 1996). One mother said that, although they only functioned as a 'normal family' when their child with learning disabilities was away, his brothers did not want him to go into residential care. A constant theme, particularly where the 'special' child was active, was that he spoiled siblings' games and made it difficult for a brother or sister to bring friends home, which ran alongside the converse theme that a child with disabilities learned from siblings and was helped by them. One study (Simeonnson & Bailey, 1986) suggests that younger siblings generally may fare worse, particularly if male, although, again, this may be true to some extent of younger brothers and sisters in many other families.

Assessment

Barr (1999) indicates that relationships with professionals are built on successful early contacts and have a lasting impact on the ability of a family to adapt. Schreiber (1984) points to the importance of a holistic approach to the family – that is, in Gambrill's (1983) words, an ecological assessment, where all family members' needs are considered within their natural environment – including a consideration of risk factors where siblings are concerned. Dale (1996) discusses the difficulty of balancing differing needs when undertaking assessments, comprising the importance of considering the family as a whole, while allowing time to listen to each member in order to ensure that each individual need is registered.

Powell & Ogle (1985) studied at length the needs of siblings in families where there was a child with disabilities and found that such siblings have many concerns which embrace worries about their 'special' brother or sister, their parents, themselves, friends, school and adulthood. They consider, and we agree, that siblings can have intense feelings about their situation and, in common with their parents, many unanswered questions. They, too, need to have the opportunity to talk to someone about their fears and feelings. Where there are only two children in the family, one source of sharing thoughts is unavailable (Murray & Jampolsky, 1982).

Despite this evidence, it would be an error to assume professional help is needed in all cases where siblings are concerned. Such a stance is potentially oppressive. Practitioner sensitivity to brothers' and sisters' own helping networks and choices is an essential part of the assessment. Nevertheless, siblings, we feel, do need special consideration, for while adjustments may well be made in the family home, sibling experiences away from home, at school or elsewhere, will, from the evidence we have reviewed, be potentially testing for them. Moreover, they may be slow to share their worries with their parents, as some of our examples show. Care taken to obtain a clear picture of the family will reveal such situations (Sloper & Turner, 1991). If offered with sensitivity, support services reduce stress, a common-sense view confirmed in Utting's (1995) report on supporting families.

Young carers

If parents have to spend more of their time in dealing with the needs of a child with disabilities, then it is not only likely that brothers and sisters will receive less attention from them, but also more likely that they will be called upon to perform parent surrogate roles. McHale & Gamble (1987) found that girl siblings could be the most stressed because they were more likely than boys to be expected to carry out such responsibilities. Sisters, particularly older sisters, according to

Lobato (1983), are likely to be expected to undertake child-sitting and domestic work, while Sourkes (1990) indicates that they may be resentful of their parents' time being directed to their disabled brother or sister. These findings may, of course, be indicative of gender and age differences in the amount of household and caring responsibilities carried out by girls and boys (and later by men and women: see Evandrou, 1990; Hubert, 1991). Thompson (1995) is concerned that young carers are denied their childhood by the nature of their caring responsibilities and stresses their need for support and counselling, as does Becker *et al.* (1998), who look at the strategy of helping young carers as a unique group as well as through support for the whole family.

The Carers National Association estimates the numbers of young carers in Britain at about 10 000. This estimate not only concerns siblings who help care for children with disabilities, but those who look after parents, who may have special needs themselves, requiring their children to care for them. It is apparent, therefore, that children do undertake adult roles for which they are ill-prepared. The Department of Health (1999), in a recent report on carers, and the earlier Carers (Recognition and Services) Act 1995 have reinforced the need to place greater emphasis on support and resources to avoid statutory intervention in families where young carers take on the main caring responsibility. This need is especially important for families where there is a child with disabilities, because an element of risk must exist when an immature individual attempts tasks beyond their ability to manage, no matter how determined that young person might be. Becker *et al.* (1998) convey the urgency of the plight of young carers, concluding that they represent a major area for preventive social work interventions.

In the next example, a younger brother and sister have developed good coping skills with their brother with learning disabilities, but uncertainties about his future are a pressure shared by the whole family.

CASE EXAMPLE: **John, Amy and Alan**

Alan is 13 years of age, his brother John is nine and his sister Amy six. Alan cannot speak but is fully mobile. In some respects his parents consider him to be autistic, although this is not a confirmed diagnosis. As a young child, he was referred to hospital, where parental concerns about his 'absences' were revealed to be a form of mild epileptic fits. Following a brain scan, his parents were informed that Alan would have some degree of learning disabilities but the full extent of these was uncertain. His father feels that Alan's diagnosis should have been made earlier, with the offer of some prognosis for the future. However, he recognises that it may have been a deliberate medical decision not to offer a prognosis if doctors think that parents are unable to cope with its impact, or if they genuinely feel unable to give more precise information at the time.

Currently, Alan's odd behaviour in public causes sidelong glances from other parents, as if to imply that he should be controlled, since he looks 'normal'. His repetitive behaviour includes getting out of bed at night and going to his parents' bedroom, saying 'out of bed' and laughing. He will repeat this behaviour as often as possible; it causes much tension because he will not stop. Alan attends a school about 50 miles away, returning home two nights a week and alternating weekends.

John and Amy take little notice of their brother's behaviour and seem to accept him as just another family member. They enjoy playing with him, tolerating his 'special games', like jumping over his sister when she lies flat on the ground. He is good at this and Amy reports that he 'never misses'.

The family's greatest concern is about Alan's future, for although the family seems to accept their current situation and outwardly appears fully functioning, they remain uncertain about what will happen when he leaves school. Future uncertainties, however, have not hindered day-to-day adjustment. There is no doubt that Alan's brother and sister find their parents supportive of them, while all family members work as a team to meet Alan's needs.

Comment

It could be argued that some delay in giving parents the 'news' about their child would enable them to learn to love the child first without letting the label of 'learning disability' get in the way. Parents might not cope if told at birth that they will always have to care for their child who might, for instance, never be able to talk. Parents might be daunted by such views. At such times, it is rare for thought to be given to how other members of the family will cope.

Sibling relationships often manifest a natural acceptance of their brother or sister. Children do not have adult expectations of what he or she should be like, rather accepting their brother or sister for what he or she is: a member of the family. On the other hand, as we have said, from an early age children need age-appropriate explanations and information about the disability in question.

The home–school distance may be a helping factor for some families. It offers a logical justification for overnight stays which serve as respite care for the family as well as relieving the child concerned from long, tiring journeys. Curtailment of these arrangements is often part of parents' fears for the future.

As in the family described, siblings benefit from parental attention during the disabled child's absences, improving their familial relationships at home. The probable benefits are of increased affection for their brother, with whom they may spend more time, willingly, when he is at home. Whatever the situation, siblings think that their parents should make time for them (Mayer & Vadasy, 1997).

Conclusion

The position of siblings in the family does require attention in its own right. Having a disabled child as a brother or sister offers in itself both advantages and disadvantages – these fluctuate with time and circumstance – but brings anxieties for the sibling concerned. Picture books, relating in story form the experiences of children with a variety of disabilities, such as those produced by Franklin Watts (96–98 Leonard Street, London EC2A 4RH), may help younger siblings understand their situation. Most siblings develop insight into the needs of disabled children, and are concerned for their future.

In many cases, as we have seen, siblings are also carers (Burke & Montgomery, 2000). Whether caring is directly or indirectly required of them, they may well feel that it is their duty to help care for their disabled brother or sister both through affection and through a wish to share their parents' perceived responsibilities. This points towards the need to allow siblings the opportunity to share their feelings and experiences.

Siblings' needs should receive attention as part of a holistic assessment of the family situation. A multi-agency, 'one door' approach (see Chapter 10) can cater for all the family's various needs, including the need for siblings to share their worries and experiences with other children in similar situations (Cigno & Gore, 1998). The essential element is that siblings need to be heard, requiring professional alertness and active listening (Towell, 1997). Assisting the family by recognising individual strengths and deficits enables decisions to be made with understanding and, as Jones (1998) comments in an essay on the place of early intervention, is a step towards empowerment and self-determination.

Chapter 7

Life Transitions and Barriers to Change

The impact of change will vary according to the individual. When a major change, involving a move from one situation or state to another, takes place it is more accurately described as a transition. For example, in Chapter 2 we noted that becoming a parent is a major point of transition. The experience of growing up through the stages of adolescence includes physical, emotional and cognitive changes as part of the transition to adulthood. Research shows that major changes induce stress, because new experiences are often associated with uncertainty and fear of the unknown; what Jones (1998) refers to as a dynamic transition. It is worth reminding ourselves that it is perfectly normal to experience an increase in stress when situations change. In this chapter, we consider how families experience transitions and how in most cases carers and children can be helped to prepare and plan for them.

Preparation for change can help alleviate some, although not all, of the stress that change brings about. Another way to alleviate stress is to prevent change. Sometimes prevention may seem preferable to responding once predictable distress has occurred (see Burke 1997a; Burke *et al.*, 1997). However, some situations cannot or should not be prevented as, for instance, the transition from childhood to adolescence and then on to adulthood, with all the risks this nevertheless entails for the child and family. In other words, a certain amount of turbulence is inherent in life transitions; feelings of stress are to be expected and are healthy. Again, some life-changing events are usually looked forward to, as when adults await the birth of their first baby, and thus the transition to parenthood. Whether the transition is eagerly sought or not, it is usually helpful if it can be anticipated and therefore managed. Below we discuss the role of antenatal tests and diagnosis in this context.

Responding to change

Reactions to change and the stress induced can be understood more readily by considering extreme situations, particularly the ensuing trauma and the stages of reactions leading to some form of adjustment or accommodation. It is helpful to understand how people initially respond to change, because we need to build up our knowledge of initial reactions to see how, with the passage of time, this reaction itself changes. The sense of loss following a bereavement can be likened to many situations when at times overwhelming feelings are faced by people undergoing significant change in their lives. Where expectations are not met, stress results. This often occurs when an experience cannot be anticipated or where some unexpected event disrupts one's life.

The Holmes and Rahe social readjustment scale (Hopson, 1981) shows that levels of stress vary according to the type of transition. To provide some indication of the degree of readjustment that is necessary, the death of a spouse is scored at 100. This compares with 50 for marriage and 39 for the birth of a child. These scores are intended to reflect the degree of stress experienced; the higher the score, the greater the stress. Scores are standardised, but the effect of any transition will vary for each individual because of the variability of stressors at play. Most people do not experience one stress at a time, but many stresses which may accumulate to produce a high score, while some minor event might trigger a stress reaction due to the intensity of an earlier, unresolved difficulty. The scale is useful because it conveys a sense of proportion; it indicates that stressful events can accumulate to the point of dysfunction, with an accumulated score of about 150 as the threshold beyond which stress is not bearable. It is therefore important to understand how individuals react to situations that promote excessive stress reactions.

Kübler-Ross (1969) was concerned with reactions to bereavement, although much of what she says is also relevant to other kinds of loss. Bereavement follows the loss of a loved one and will trigger reflections about missed opportunities as well as shared, happy moments; such reflections can be both painful and pleasurable for the bereaved individual. Children with multiple disabilities may experience conditions which are life-shortening (Closs, 1998) and some will receive care in the hospice sector (Burke, 1991), such that proximity to the immediacy of death is a preparation for anticipated bereavement. Matthew's mother expressed her thoughts about the future thus:

'We live our lives on a day-to-day basis, making the best of what we have, not knowing what tomorrow will bring. Matthew does not understand his life-threatening condition, but we know he is happy and he really enjoys the presence of his family.'

The life-shortening experience is yet another major transition faced by children themselves. Perhaps the best way parents can manage is to make the most of the time available and, rather than learning to regret, use such time for playing and sharing activities. We are informed that Matthew is able to enjoy his food, the company of other children and television (probably in that order) and smiles a great deal; yet he cannot speak, is partially sighted, cannot use his limbs, and may not have long to live.

Kübler-Ross (1969) identified five major reactive stages: denial, anger, bargaining, depression and acceptance. In order to achieve some form of acceptance, a person who is bereaved has to come to terms with their experience. There is a sense of working through each of the stages to achieve a level of acceptance. The reality, however, is that people do not progress to acceptance necessarily in a linear and orderly fashion; and some may never accept the loss of someone they once loved.

The grief of bereavement is about feelings of loss. This initial reaction is similar for people who learn that their child has learning disabilities. A sense of loss, shock, even disbelief are common feelings experienced by parents who face, for the first time, the fact that their child is different in unexpected ways. The parent who hears that their newborn infant is disabled is likely to have a different reaction from one who discovers this later. Early reactions are likely to follow those of the 'bereavement cycle', with sorrow for what might have been. When disability is undetected, parents will usually welcome their child as a joyous event and only later need to make a fundamental readjustment to their ideas of the child's future needs (Dyson, 1996). In such cases, problems are likely to arise out of concern for remedy rather than from difficulties in accepting the child for what he or she is.

In our 1995 study (Burke & Cigno, 1996), which looked at the adjustments made by families with children with learning disabilities, we showed that people often reach a stage of accommodation to their experience rather than an acceptance of it. An adjustment to one's situation recognises that painful reflections will take place, with flashbacks to what might have been not uncommon but this does not imply that an individual has fully accepted their lot. In fact, the experience of families is such that they consider themselves from then on as 'disabled families' operating within a system that is different from other families. They have to take account of new contingencies which often highlight the barriers and difficulties of caring for a child with learning disabilities. The impact on children themselves of learning about their disability is also intense but far less well documented. It may be better understood by applying a 'change/life cycle model' (Dale, 1996, p. 115) which looks at the impact of change over time and the need for different kinds of support that individual family members might require.

Diagnosis and detection: effects on parents

Over the last couple of decades, there have been huge changes in the amount of information available to pregnant women (particularly in the western world) through antenatal tests. Not only do antenatal tests influence choices about pregnancies, pre-conception genetic testing is also widely available, allowing prospective parents the possibility, within the boundaries of prevailing ethics and circumstances, to decide whether to conceive children at all. Such early information and diagnosis is certainly useful but also brings in its wake more than one dilemma; if the likelihood of producing a disabled child is high and the parents, or the mother alone, decide to take that risk and go ahead with the pregnancy, it could be argued that their commitment to their child will be the greater, whatever the outcome. On the other hand, for a variety of reasons, the realisation of the prospect of bearing a disabled child might bring with it unexpected reactions, and an early termination of pregnancy might be a consequence.

Some of our earlier research provided a small number of cases where the parents were aware prior to the birth that their child would have a learning disability. We were able to talk only to mothers about this; as we have said earlier, the probability is that the reactions of fathers would be more negative. However, one father, whose partner decided not to have an antenatal test, and subsequently gave birth to a Down's child, expressed his initial doubts about his ability to love his daughter, but later came to treat her equally with other children in his family (see Chapter 2).

One mother of a Down's child had received the diagnosis during pregnancy (following an amniocentesis diagnostic procedure which is used to examine amniotic fluid, withdrawn by a needle, during the 16th to 18th week of gestation). She was positive about giving birth to her daughter, an attitude which she still retained after 15 years. Two other mothers, one also of a Down's child and the other of a child with a genetically inherited condition, did not believe in abortion and therefore 'had no choice' but to go ahead with the pregnancy after being given the diagnosis. Several years later, when their children were in their teens, they still felt profound sorrow at the changes in their lives brought about by learning disability in the family. For other parents for whom the alternative option is available – termination of the pregnancy – then the moral ground is difficult and still remains difficult to resolve, as it does for doctors as well as others not directly involved but concerned about such decisions.

It is impossible to say whether the lives of the children concerned would have been better or worse without antenatal diagnosis. The area of the effects of antenatal detection on the subsequent lives of children is important, and one which would benefit from more exploration from a social and emotional standpoint.

When a child is diagnosed as learning-disabled following birth, the sense of bereavement reflects the loss of the 'normal' baby whom the parents expected. This sensation may cause parents to feel guilt, first because they fear that they may have somehow contributed to the child's condition, and second because they may feel that their sense of disappointment blames the child for something that is not his or her fault. Following the initial shock, families have to come to terms with the situation and face the fact that their expectations prior to the birth of the child might no longer be appropriate. The family has to adjust its lifestyle to meet the needs of their child and to help all family members cope with the situation (Abbott & Sapsford, 1988). However, when the detection of a learning disability occurs some time later, either because it is not immediately detectable, or through disease or accident then, although the child is already an integrated part of the family, the sense of loss – certainly unfairness – might be greater.

The following case examples compare and contrast different situations regarding initial diagnosis, subsequent developments and the realisation of the impact and extent of disability on parents and, especially as the years go by, on the children and young people themselves.

CASE EXAMPLE: **Robert**

Robert, aged seven, is the eldest of four children. He has two sisters, aged six and two, and a brother of five years. He lives with his parents in a three-bedroomed council house.

Robert was born following an emergency Caesarean section during which an artery was severed. He appears to have suffered brain injury as a result. No admission of medical negligence was ever made and the parents feel unable to pursue such matters. His siblings are in all respects 'normal'.

Robert has severe learning disabilities and, although fully ambulant, his visual acuity is defective: he can only perceive objects within a few metres. Robert also has hearing difficulties, but he can express his needs verbally. He wears nappies and needs adult supervision at night as he is likely to remove his nappy and wet the bed. His memory for following the simplest of instructions is very limited. He lacks awareness of danger and exhibits what his parents describe as 'challenging behaviour'. His behaviour on any family outing tends to result in disapproving looks from other families, suggesting that the parents are to blame for a badly behaved child.

Robert's parents felt that they were not offered much in the way of support and advice from professionals during the early days when their son's survival was in question. They have always used each other as a major source of support. Extended family help was not available, as both sets of grandparents live some distance away, and so their experience was of isolation from other family members.

Comment

Children with learning disabilities may experience developmental delays (see Chapter 3) and, as in the case of Robert, such a diagnosis, although unspecific, may help parents adjust from the outset to a major transition. The degree of Robert's learning disabilities was only revealed as he grew older, when it became apparent that he was not managing to achieve milestones at an age-appropriate level, but by this time he had been accepted and was loved by his parents. Anger tends to be directed towards professionals 'who should have done more to help' rather than at themselves or the child.

Whatever the cause of Robert's difficulties, his parents blame the medical profession due to problems which occurred at birth. They do, however, accept the consequences as they see them: they must care for their son as well as they can. They have also proved to themselves that they can produce 'normal' children since they have gone on to have three more children, although this, too, reinforces their belief that had circumstances surrounding his birth been different, Robert would not have been born with disabilities. The reality is that Robert has special needs, and his parents have accepted him, though their anger has yet to be resolved, since caring for him is experienced as a daily trial.

Since they cope and manage their day-to-day lives, it could be said that they have reached a high level of adjustment, although they still feel powerless as they struggle to contain their bitterness about doctors. The transition of becoming carers has become a continuum of care, a permanent condition, and although his parents have improved their caring skills, they continue to be concerned about new challenges in Robert's life on an almost daily basis as well as to worry about his future.

Physical and emotional barriers

When any parent takes a baby or toddler out in a pram to go shopping, there is a degree of inconvenience due to the restrictions in many shops where doors can be opened and closed only with difficulty, and doorways and aisles are narrow. Other common barriers are steps, roadside kerbs and crowds along busy high streets. This is a familiar enough experience for most parents, even though nowadays the use of prams is increasingly tolerated by the public and shopkeepers. However, many children with learning disabilities also have mobility problems and continue to rely on larger versions of prams or buggies for outings. The users of special transport equipment encounter daily physical barriers for children and families due to its size and manoeuvrability. More important still, like an adult wheelchair, it also presents a clear sign of disability, labelling its occupant as uncomfortably different.

Many barriers are not as obvious as physical ones. Barriers limiting choice may also be social, psychological or communicative. These might just as effectively exclude vulnerable people from obtaining access to services, or from feeling that they are participating in or making a choice about their care. For instance, a barrier which is created by negative attitudes towards learning disability is likely to be just as, if not more, difficult to change than environmental obstacles. The following example illustrates how professionals can themselves allow low expectations to influence assessment and therefore act unwittingly as a barrier to a child's progress.

CASE EXAMPLE: **Douglas**

Douglas is a four-year-old boy who has cerebral palsy. He cannot walk unaided, but can shuffle about on his hands and knees. At nursery school, he manages to walk short distances using a rollator (a zimmer frame-type device with wheels at the front to ease movement of the frame).

Douglas's intellectual ability is uncertain, although his parents say that he is inquisitive, enjoys straightforward computer games and likes to watch television. He speaks in simple sentences and has a cheerful disposition. He enjoys cuddles, although he is less confident with men, or 'mens' as he calls them, perhaps because, like most children, he attends a nursery staffed only by women. When it came to the time for Douglas's statement of special needs, a male educational psychologist was assigned to test him. The educational psychologist met Douglas at his new school, which it was thought would meet his needs after nursery (a privately run establishment with a good reputation). The psychologist had only met Douglas on one previous occasion.

He had therefore at least two barriers to overcome: first, the adjustment to a new school, which was large in comparison with his nursery experience; and second, his own uncertainty in the presence of male strangers. Further, the psychologist, who was business-like in his manner, and probably intimidating to a child, did not appear to relish 'play' as an activity appropriate for testing children despite having to use toys as part of the assessment procedure. It seems that the psychologist judged Douglas's physical condition as a reflection of his mental abilities and therefore anticipated a low level of achievement in test scores. He did little to make the child feel at ease.

Douglas scored in the lowest centile ranking on the standardised test. Dissatisfied, the child's parents requested a second opinion. Further tests carried out in his own home by a female psychologist, who took time to get to know him by sitting on the floor, talking and playing, confirmed that the child was in the low average range of ability. The original test had misrepresented his abilities, demonstrating how environments can present barriers to communication and performance.

Comment

The child's disability influenced the first psychologist's perceptions of the child's abilities and consequently the child's performance. Had the child been treated as a child first, as was his right in actual and natural law, then it is likely that he would have performed much better. This example may be extreme, but if Douglas's parents had not protested and requested a second opinion, his poor performance would have been accepted, with consequences for his immediate and perhaps future life chances. A child and his family, therefore, may encounter barriers to progress in the professional's study as well as in the streets and shops. The entire area of the removal of barriers for disabled children has recently been the subject of a report by the Social Services Inspectorate (SSI) (1998c).

Transitions to school

Douglas had experienced some preparation for education, common to many children, by attending a nursery school. Most children with learning disabilities will now have this experience, since they are given priority in pre-school education; many will also have had the advantage of involvement with the home-based, step-by-step teaching system, Portage, extremely popular with parents (see Lloyd, 1986, for a detailed account of how this works).

However, Douglas's move to special school, combined with his lack of familiarity with men in a school environment, had caused him to underfunction during psychological testing. Transitions are by their nature stressful and children, like adults, do not perform as well when undue stress influences their ability to function normally. Labels, even when wrongly attributed, tend to stick, as the Warnock Report (1978) commented, resulting in persistent stigmatisation.

Children with learning disabilities experience transitions like everyone else, except their capacity is impaired to some extent by their intellectual and physical restrictions. It might be considered, therefore, that they will find change and new experiences more difficult to grasp, an essential point for professional awareness. Many of us have been in the position of taking a child to school on his or her very first day, as well as observing other children in a like position. Expressed emotion (of the children, though occasionally of the parents!) runs the full range in any group from smiles, pouts, poker-face, tears, sobs and screams. A child who understands less well what is happening may be especially disadvantaged.

The situation for children with learning disabilities at the point of school entry is additionally framed by education policy concerning children with special needs. The medical model of disability, according to Oliver & Barnes (1998), still dominates, the consequence of which is that children are 'treated' (in a medical sense) and treatment requires special remedies. Consequently, special schools are provided to serve special children, and usually do so, but also segregate them from mainstream opportunities available to other children. This could lead to an oppression of such children, if their needs are not being served and they are instead being 'put away'. However, choice is the important factor, for a special school, after careful assessment, might be the appropriate place to meet a child's needs.

The alternative of inclusive education in mainstream schools can also be found wanting, particularly if children do not fully participate in mainstream classes, although there is evidence that 'located' units in mainstream schools, with partial integration, have some merits, but are currently out of favour (see Burke & Cigno, 1996, for a discussion of educational alternatives, particularly of 'located' units in mainstream primaries). Whatever the school setting, staff need to be able to teach children daily living skills which will help lead them to independence (Baker & Brightman, 1997).

Kidd & Hornby (1993) write on this theme in their discussion of transition to inclusion in mainstream schools. We suggest that integration is a more meaningful concept, involving individual identity with the group, but the question of how integration is achieved without loss of a child's individuality is a problem common to both mainstream and special schools. The drive towards inclusive education that fully integrates children with learning difficulties is more disputed than inclusive education for children with physical disabilities, even though the latter require considerable support in order to avoid disadvantage and discrimination in school.

It could be argued that some learning-disabled children flourish in special schools that can provide opportunities for their development not available in the mainstream sector, even with additional support. There is, too, a small amount of evidence that children leaving special schools are better served by support services (Young Adults Transition Project (YATP), 1998, 1999). One mother of a 10-year-old girl, after a great deal of thought and discussion with her daughter, transferred her to a special school 'so at least she can have the experience of shining instead of always being at the bottom'. And, as we have pointed out elsewhere in this book, the availability of a flexible hostel facility at some special schools is a big attraction to many families and a strong factor in decision-making.

A parental view is not necessarily identical with the child's wishes, but parental responsibility in making choices for children over the transition into school is generally accepted for all children. Nevertheless, gradual child involvement with decisions is an important training towards eventual independence. Sands & Wehmeyer (1996) show that early involvement in decision-making encourages involvement in later decisions, a sense of involvement, and an increase in self-awareness. The child's right to be involved can easily be overlooked at this significant time, when carers, education officials, teachers, psychologists and often other professionals are all trying to do their best for the child.

Transitions from school to adulthood

If going to school as an infant is an anxious time for children and families, leaving school at 16+ is often a time of crisis, anticipated for many years by parents. Leaving school occurs at a time when biological changes of adolescence are also taking place. Families tell us that they have little preparation for the move; and few, apparently, are aware of the rights of special needs young people to continuing education. Riddell (1998) discusses the markers of adulthood, and comments on the age-specific thresholds which have to be crossed:

> 'These thresholds include criminal responsibility, sexual consent, voting rights, conditional or unconditional marriage rights, the right to enter full-time paid or unpaid employment, the right to welfare benefits, to give or withhold medical consent and to donate blood or organs'

> (p. 194).

Young learning-disabled people should be treated equally as regards opportunities. This is the sense of the Disability Discrimination Act 1995, but opportunities for young people seeking employment are limited by state policy set to promote education and training in the 16–18 age group generally. Evidence to this effect was provided earlier by May & Hughes (1985) in their study of young people leaving special school. One consequence still is that the tendency is to seek further education or attend special school-leaver training schemes (Riddell, 1998). This finding is confirmed by the Young Adults Transition Project (1999), a large, long-term project taking place in some London boroughs. The researchers found that many disabled school leavers would prefer a job, but few found one; and that for many young people there was little planning, information and follow-up.

The next case example is one of a solution being found, but not to the satisfaction of the family.

CASE EXAMPLE: **Graham**

Graham, aged 16, used to live at home with his sister (21), mother and stepfather. He is diagnosed as autistic, although this was only recently clarified, for he was previously labelled as having 'global developmental delay'. His sister has disabilities resulting from brain injury following a viral infection in infancy. Graham requires 24-hour care to keep him safe and his behaviour under control. He is at risk to himself if not constantly supervised. The parents describe their situation as being 'under constant stress'.

Recently, Graham left home to attend a residential school more than 70 miles away. The original plan, according to the school review, was that he should remain at the local school, utilising the attached hostel for frequent weekday and occasional weekend respite care, until he reached 19. However, the post-16 educational provision at the school changed; the alternative offered did not have residential facilities and so the opportunity for respite care was not available. Both parents refused to agree to the proposed change since they felt that Graham's needs were best met by a local school with residential care facilities.

After persistent pressure from the parents, the LEA agreed to offer an out-of-area facility at a residential college subject to a six-month assessment. However, the new educational provision, while catering for Graham's educational needs, is at a considerable distance from his home. From the family's point of view, this would have all kinds of repercussions. His father commented:

> 'If Graham should learn to speak any more words he won't have a local accent – it's not right. Graham goes where he is sent – it's disgusting.'

Although to an outsider the presence or otherwise of a local accent might be a relatively trivial matter, emotionally such concerns are significant barriers, compounding the geographical ones, to the child–parent bond.

Comment

Autism is a condition that is difficult to understand and one where the transition to adulthood is particularly hard to manage for the young person and his or her family. Because specialist care and education is often required, the effect of transfer from one school to another and from one part of the country to another may increase the stress experienced by the child and family, as the above example shows.

The lack of information and uncertainties about further education made the change in the original transitional plans difficult to grasp (Burke 1997a). Consequently, both parents felt that their son was offered an unsuitable service due to resource problems which did not take into account all his needs. The original alternative to his previous school might easily have been accepted had both parents not persevered, because they felt that Graham and the whole family would have suffered from the withdrawal of respite care. The importance of different kinds of out-of-home care for children with disabilities is examined in reports by the SSI (Social Services Inspectorate 1997, 1998b). Here, as in other situations, the question of choice as a means of giving power to families is a crucial factor.

Leaving school, transferring to further education, an adult training centre or some form of employment happens during adolescence, a time when young people are especially sensitive to their own image and to relationships. The following example concerns Kevin, who was struggling with many issues facing young people in their late teens.

CASE EXAMPLE: **Kevin**

Kevin, nearly 17, lives with his mother, a single parent, a younger brother, Ross, aged ten, and two older sisters, Rosie and Lesley, aged 19 and 20, respectively. There is another older, married sister living nearby. An uncle, the mother's brother, also lives near, offering practical help to the family by carrying out household maintenance. Kevin has no contact with his father, who left the family eight years ago. The family lives in council property, surviving for many years on benefits and allowances. The atmosphere is easygoing. Kevin is very attached to his family and they to him.

According to his mother, Kevin's development slowed down after a fire at the house when he was six. He never recovered, remaining 'behind' ever since. He is a tall, good-looking young man who speaks slowly with hesitation.

Kevin is due to leave (special) school soon. His mother says that recently he has been worrying about his future. She thinks that perhaps there has been some 'talk' about independence at school. As they walk through the estate, if he spots an empty flat, he says, 'I could live there.' He also says, 'I'll get married one day.'

His sisters 'take him with them everywhere', including 'clubbing'. He has tried to approach girls 'who are attracted to him until they hear him speak, then they won't dance with him'. This upsets him, and for a while afterwards he refuses to go out.

His mother worries about what to do for the best. She feels that he is unrealistic in his aspirations to live independently, get a job, have a girlfriend, perhaps get married. On reflection, she thinks that he has been too sheltered until now by her and his sisters, because he will not find this love and tolerance elsewhere. She wonders what will happen to him, and if she is to blame for protecting him.

Comment

Kevin's close, affectionate family has not prepared him for the difficulties and rebuffs he is beginning to face as an adult. His mother does not seek help, and is wary of 'the authorities' due to past experiences when she struggled to bring up a family in the midst of conflict with her ex-husband and an uncertain income. It seems as if teachers at school have begun to explore some issues with Kevin, but the other members of his family are only vaguely aware of what is going on. As school is the only institution tolerated by the family (they have a poor opinion of social workers who 'never told us about allowances and things'), teachers would probably be in the best position to reach out to the family to help them support Kevin more appropriately, exploring together what resources are available to help him into adulthood.

The many studies on this topic, and local authority initiatives now taking place with young adults with learning disabilities, are witness to the crucial nature of understanding and planning for this transition (Baker & Brightman, 1997; Social Services Inspectorate, 1998a,b; McIntosh & Whittaker, 1998; Wertheimer, 1998; Young Adults Transition Project, 1998, 1999).

Conclusion

Times of transition bring extra worries and stress for families. Professionals need to understand that at these stages children and parents need more information, consultation and support. Such support is usually best offered and coordinated initially from the place where the change is taking place; thus, when a child with learning disabilities is born, this support would immediately be offered by professionals situated at the hospital. Subsequently, a keyworker approach would help continuity of support over the years and through life changes, although other professionals from trusted institutions still have an important part to play. When the transition can be anticipated, as when a child starts school or a young person approaches school-leaving age, then families can be helped to prepare gradually. At the present time, professional support appears to be patchy: it is there for some families but not for others; it is present in some geographical areas and not others; it is available at some times and not others. Help in overcoming barriers and managing change is fundamental for families where there is a child with learning disabilities. It should not be left to chance or individual circumstances.

Chapter 8

Child Protection: Prevention and Risk

Throughout this book, we stress that children with learning disabilities share the experiences of other children. This may mean that they suffer abuse and neglect and therefore also need the same protection from abusers. However, the precursors and consequences may not be the same as those for other children, and they merit special attention. These points concerning differences within an overall inclusive approach to safeguarding children are also highlighted in the new government guidance on working together (Department of Health, Home Office, Department for Education and Employment, 1999). For instance, the guidance refers to the evidence that disabled children may have fewer external contacts than other children, be more vulnerable to peer abuse and, because they often need intimate personal care, are more exposed to the risk of abuse. The guidance makes more than one reference to the particular concerns where children have communication difficulties (section 6.26–6.29).

According to Westcott (1998), children with disabilities may be considered 'ideal victims' by the potential abuser. The research evidence from Cross *et al.* (1993) indicates that disabled children were nearly twice as likely to be abused than non-disabled children. Therefore a double jeopardy exists, because while all children are subject to the power and influence of others (usually their carers, informal and formal), and therefore vulnerable to abuse, children with disabilities are potentially further at risk because, particularly if they have moderate to severe learning disabilities, they may find it difficult to communicate their experiences (Kennedy, 1992; Mencap, 1999). In addition, since they bear the label 'disabled' they are often less listened to, understood or believed than non-disabled children. However, many people find it difficult to believe that disabled children may be targets of abusers (Kennedy, 1995), thus rendering them ideal victims for perpetrators. Furthermore, as Westcott &

Cross (1996) explain, disabled and learning-disabled people are sometimes considered as inviting or provoking abuse. In other words, perpetrators may be at least partially exonerated. Such a view is often called victim-blaming. Vulnerability here is twofold: first, the risk of being abused, and second, being blamed for the abuse.

In this chapter, we explore the need for child protection services, the role of preventive and supportive work and the element of risk and stigma which may result from social work intervention itself.

Prevention

Policies and practice directed at preventing abuse happening or escalating are to be preferred to risk assessments and investigation after suspected or actual abuse has taken place. In a social and medical context, the word 'prevention' has for most people positive connotations. In social policy, we have borrowed from medicine the distinctions between primary, secondary and tertiary prevention and sought to apply them (with varying success) to social situations (Burke 1997b). In the field of child abuse, for example, primary prevention means stopping 'it' happening at all; better education for parenting is one instance. Secondary prevention may refer to 'catching it' in time and stopping it 'spreading' within a family. After more abuse has occurred or seems imminent, then the strategy will be directed at supporting parents to avoid its recurrence. Tertiary prevention recognises that serious abuse has taken place but seeks to reduce its traumatic effects by therapy or counselling, for example, or, as a last resort, by 'removing' the 'damaged' child. These distinctions are not clear-cut and there are difficulties in applying the medical model in social affairs, but they afford a useful way of clearing the ground in a conceptually complex case (Hardiker *et al.*, 1991; Stevenson, 1998; and see Hardiker, 1996, for a more sophisticated account of threshold criteria between one level and another and of legal interpretations of significant harm). Of late, the Department of Health has sought to redress the balance in child care practice so that more effort and resources may be put into supporting children 'in need' under the terms of the Children Act 1989. It is generally agreed that the spirit of the Act was not fully realised when the lion's share of resources went towards formal investigations of abuse.

Under the Children and Young Persons Act 1969, prevention policies in social work centred on keeping families together by avoiding reception of children into care, providing that their welfare was not dangerously compromised. Packman (1981) observes that, from the 1950s until the late 1960s, the concept of prevention concerned both the need to prevent cruelty and neglect and the need to prevent children going into the care system (p. 58). This produced a potential conflict of interest in cases of child abuse when prevention of abuse required the child to enter care. Social workers continue, to some extent, to struggle with the meaning of prevention (see Burke *et al.*, 1997) given that its conceptualisation has become increasingly broad.

Some of the central difficulties in translating ideals of prevention into reality were the imprecision of the term, uncertainty about some of the goals and uncertainty about criteria for the evaluation of success and failure and how to measure these. Without greater precision, the resource implications were alarmingly unclear. It is therefore not surprising that the terminology shifted to talk about 'family support'. However, this still leaves us with a political and social dilemma: how 'universal' or 'selective' should such family support be? 'Universal' policies usually fall under the primary prevention head, 'selective' policies are more likely to be in the framework of secondary or tertiary prevention. These policy discussions are particularly important in the area of children with learning disabilities. 'Universal' policies of family support are attractive for their avoidance of stigma but the resource implications are heavy.

Behind all family policies enshrined in the Children Act 1989 are two assumptions: first, that the welfare of the child is paramount; second, that, wherever possible, professionals should be working 'in partnership' with parents to that end. In the phrase 'wherever possible', however, lies the heart of the dilemmas which professionals must somehow seek to resolve, for there will be a small number of occasions where the child's interests cannot be safeguarded via the parents. In extreme cases, a child will have to be removed. But this action may not guarantee their safety. One of the tragedies of child welfare is the revelation of the abuse of children in residential care over the past 30 years (Utting, 1997; Department of Health, 2000).

Amidst all the debate about the efficacy of 'preventive' and support strategies, what is certain is that families with a learning-disabled child appreciate support services. Furthermore, their ethical justification seems indisputable. Recent research on effectiveness attempts to discover which approaches and services are effective in which situation, with which people and with which problems

(Cigno, 1995b; Sheldon, 1995). Cigno (1995b) and Burke (1998a), for example, examines the evidence supporting the use of intervention based on learning theories in family situations where safeguarding children is an issue. Such approaches also give weight to the quality of life factor; that is, whether actual harm would have occurred or not, enhancing a child's development and environment is good practice and is part of a non-stigmatising approach to formal child care provision. It is probably no coincidence that evidence-based practice is currently and belatedly given more prominence within both health and social care.

Assessments of need are part of the duties of health, social and educational professionals who have legal powers to identify and act in respect of people whom they perceive as needing support or being at risk of harm. In the latter case, all such assessments can be seen as part of preventive work in its narrower sense; they are part of a process of investigation and intervention where the aim is to minimise harm or distress.

CASE EXAMPLE: Jonathan

Jonathan is a ten-year-old Down's child. He has three older brothers. Jonathan is physically active, and likes painting and watching videos. He is prone to temper tantrums and has problems communicating his wishes. He has very limited speech but can use Makaton symbols to indicate basic needs. The family has support from maternal grandparents who run a smallholding with a number of animals. In these surroundings, Jonathan responds positively, running and playing freely. He is able to ride a horse.

Both parents expressed the shock they experienced when Jonathan was born. They felt that they needed counselling to overcome the experience but did not get this. They questioned whether they should have had Jonathan adopted at birth. Obviously, this did not happen, and later they came to love him for himself. However, they feel that their marriage would not have survived the stress of caring without the help provided by extended family and periods of respite care for Jonathan. During these times, the family (minus Jonathan) 'does things we couldn't do if he were there', sometimes taking a little holiday away.

Jonathan is not an easy child and his future needs remain uncertain. His parents admit ambivalent feelings towards him, and both feel that he should eventually go into residential care. They have investigated some possibilities, despite feelings of guilt, but his brothers do not like the idea of Jonathan's going away. Jonathan's own views are unclear, although he accepts going away for respite care.

Comment

In Jonathan's case, a conflict of interests exists. He has the right to have his interests represented under child care legislation but has limited ability to express his own needs. His skills at Makaton might augment his expression if appropriate options can be offered and he is encouraged to make a choice. At present, his parents would like him to go away from home to stay permanently in residential care, his brothers would like him to stay at home, while Jonathan has not been helped to make his views known. The parents have received the message from professionals that the norm is for a disabled child to remain at home, thus increasing their guilt and ambivalent feelings towards their son. It is probable that Jonathan would not wish to leave home, even if he could fully understand the consequences of permanent residential care.

It seems that Jonathan needs someone to represent his interests. However, if both parents wish to consider the residential option, and since many disabled people still live in residential care (Morris, 1995), then it is possible that, by remaining at home, the tensions would become excessive and the family would be in danger of dis-integration. Probably a halfway solution would be the answer, with extra hostel or respite care available during the week and some weekends, so that family unity could be maintained and the stresses of caring reduced. The difficulty is that either/or decisions polarise the realities into unrealistic choices, whereas compromise might serve all parties involved and provide a satisfactory solution.

Child protection matters

The assessment of children who are referred for child protection investigation is subject to procedures requiring medical and legal information to establish whether the cause of any injuries received is accidental or deliberate, and if the culpability for any deficits in caring lies with the child's carers. Such professional assessments may be more difficult than usual in the case of children with disabilities who may, for example, be subject to a certain amount of restraint by their carers due to their disability and therefore may not be as publicly visible as other children.

Morris (1999) puts the vulnerability of disabled children into this context. She concludes, from interviews with disabled children and young people who have experienced the child protection system, that their needs are not being met on several counts. These include, on the one hand, their over-representation on the child protection register and, on the other, the under-reporting, or non-recognition, of abusive situations regarding them: another paradox.

While urging caution over the available figures, Morris draws out further issues: there is little guidance on the interpretation of 'disabled'; gender differences affecting the category of abuse (boys being more likely to be registered under physical abuse and neglect and girls as being sexually or emotionally abused); barriers to communication with children; legal requirements not being followed when decisions on out-of-home placements are made; and lack of proper care planning and reviewing. Perhaps through fear or incompetency, there was also some evidence that social workers were avoiding contact with the child. Morris concludes that disabled children are not well served by the systems which are intended to protect them. It remains to be seen whether the new guidance (Department of Health, Home Office, Department for Education and Employment, 1999) to which we refer in the introduction to this chapter will improve these serious defects in services for disabled children. The key role assigned to area child protection committees (ACPCs) in safeguarding disabled children by raising public and professional awareness, meeting inter-agency training needs and acting as a watchdog to ensure that local policies and procedures meet such children's needs (section 6.29) gives some grounds for optimism.

Ellis & Hendry (1998) found that mainstream practitioners were not aware of, and not trained in, detecting and dealing with abuse as it affects children and adults with learning difficulties, concluding that such training should not be confined to specialists. Concerns about the sexual abuse of children with learning difficulties have led others to work with parents and children on sexuality and safety issues, a theme taken up Lee *et al.* (1998), who observe that, while awareness and safety skills in the area of sexual abuse have been brought into mainstream schools, it is only recently that professional interest has turned to children in special education. Their research addressed the effectiveness of computer-based safety programmes for these children and young people, tailored to the individual needs of the child, where imaginative and developmentally appropriate methods were used for communicating safety aware-ness and measures to the children.

Such initiatives are encouraging, providing some indication that the abuse of disabled children is being taken seriously and that child care professionals are adopting an inclusive policy, while taking into account the need for differences in approach – in assessment and communication, for example – when working with disabled chil-dren and their carers.

Risk-taking

The assessment of risk of abuse is, of course, a critical factor in child protection work. There are some situations when 'the facts' speak for themselves but even in apparently clear-cut cases, complicating evidence, such as a 'brittle bones' condition, can blur or change the assessment. This may be particularly problematic in some cases of physical disability which, as we have emphasised in the early chapters, very often accompanies learning disabilities. Furthermore, when alleged 'neglect' is an aspect of abuse, difficult questions arise concerning the balance between parental protectiveness and acceptance of the child's need to take risks.

There is also the problem of communicating effectively with children about their wishes and needs. In the case of children and young people with learning difficulties, professionals are likely to have to learn additional ways of ascertaining the child's wishes and assessing his or her situation. For instance, there is increasing recognition that people with learning disabilities may also suffer from forms of mental illness, requiring the practitioner to possess multiple skills and knowledge in the areas of legislation, recognition, assessment, the role of other professionals, appropriate intervention and resources (Dawson & Morgan, 1998). Kushlick *et al.* (1998) have written eloquently about working sensitively with learning-disabled people whose emotional state can result in challenging behaviour which may harm the person him- or herself and the carer. Although these authors' work is with adults, their guide for carers, aimed at helping them to rethink unpleasant transactions, has relevance for those caring for young people, too.

While it is unrealistic to expect a 100% success rate in social work interventions where multiple factors have to be taken into con-sideration, the success of preventive policies is, as we have said, difficult to evaluate. On the other hand, intervention based solely on an investigation of risk rather than an ecological approach to assessing the situation can be dangerous and unhelpful to child and family. There is, in fact, no reason why family support should not be offered when a child is on the child protection register or why, after careful assessment, family support should not be offered as an alternative. The following is an example of a case where the decision was taken to place a child's name on the register.

CASE EXAMPLE: **Julian**

Julian is a six-year-old boy with multiple disabilities. He is an only child. He lives with both parents on a council estate which has a poor reputation locally of being run-down. Julian's mother explains that she had difficulty giving birth to him, although no reason was found for this.

Julian is ambulant but has limited speech, resorting to gestures to indicate his wishes, particularly at mealtimes when he will point to what he wants. He attends a special school and, like Jonathan in the example given above, has some understanding of Makaton symbols, but is not at all proficient in their use.

When he was three, Julian fell down the stairs and broke his ankle. The social services department became involved and concerns were so great that his name was placed on the child protection register, following a case conference. At a recent review, it was decided that his name could be removed. Both parents feel that the experience has been very difficult for them and, while they understand the need to protect Julian and children generally, they do not think that it was the right decision to put his name on the register. They see this action as clearly blaming them for Julian's injury.

Fortunately, supportive maternal grandparents live near enough to look after Julian as and when required. The social services department has been anxious to monitor the family's progress, taking the grandparents' support into the equation, in order to ensure that Julian's safety at home is adequately safeguarded. Julian's future physical and intellectual development is uncertain.

Comment

This case demonstrates that uncertainties existed in the minds of the practitioners in the agencies involved over Julian's accident and the quality of his care at home. It is possible that his name should never have been placed on the child protection register, but because it was, a keyworker was necessarily appointed and became closely involved with the family.

Due to his level of disability, Julian was a 'child in need' under child care legislation, but this itself was not thought to be enough to safeguard his future. The investigators did not believe that the injuries he received were accidental. Even had they been accidental, they would have given rise to suspicions of neglect or lack of care. The often-encountered view that accidental injury means that there is no cause for concern is a dangerous fallacy, particularly if the accidents are repeated. Accidents can be a feature of neglect or lack of adequate surveillance. In this case, though, it appeared that the accident was an isolated incident.

Given the additional stresses in homes where parents care for disabled children, the probability that the decision to register Julian erred on the side of caution is strong, because of the known vulnerability of children like Julian. Perhaps this intervention resulted in better care for him and more family support. But this fudges the issue, which is, were the suspicions of intended harm or lack of care sufficiently strong to justify the inclusion of Julian's name on the register? Child protection registration is not the right vehicle for the provision of support services, as the authors of *Child Protection: Messages from Research* have pointed out (Department of Health, 1995). Arguably, as the incident involving Julian's fall and injury was apparently an isolated event, what the family needed was advice and support through a skilled and knowledgeable practitioner, not the stigma of child protection monitoring. The point is that the Children Act's section 47 should be used when thorough assessment indicates its appropriateness and not because otherwise support would be absent. If this section of the Act is used as the only means of providing support, then families will continue to associate social workers with child protection alone. Changes in social work practice along the lines suggested in recent Social Services Inspectorate (1997a,b; 1998a,b) reports – better assessments, for example – are needed.

Vulnerability in the community

A different kind of risk often awaits young people attempting to lead an independent social life. Again, this is true of many young people but those with learning disabilities are more vulnerable for reasons given earlier in this chapter. The exposure of adolescents to an often unsympathetic social environment can lead to the risk of actual

physical harm or blows to self-esteem, resulting in either case in fear
of 'open market' social situations and loss of confidence in the
person's ability to cope.

An example of the former is given by Burke *et al.*, (1997), where a
slightly built, gay young man living in supported housing was both
threatened and exploited when he visited his local pub. On one
occasion, he was beaten up, but he still wished to continue with his
chosen social life. The question of sexual preference also arises and
concerns the individual's right to make particular choices. Vulnerability and exclusion here may arise out of differences perceived by
others; the professional involved will need to ensure that while the
young man is not necessarily exposed to unacceptable risks from
dangerous others, he should be sufficiently empowered to maintain
his chosen lifestyle (Weston, 1991). The social services support
worker effected an improvement in the situation by arranging for
him to be accompanied on 'risky' outings by a friend who had mild
learning difficulties but, apart from being calm and burly, was also
socially skilled and practical. This solution is, of course, not focused
on changing the environment, especially the behaviour of other men
at the pub. Such a wider intervention is desirable but long term; here
the young man concerned needed immediate action to protect him
and improve his social life.

The case of Kevin, discussed more fully in Chapter 7, illustrates
the latter risk situation: exposure to rebuffs and exclusion by 'normal' peers in social situations. His family's dilemma, unresolved,
was whether to 'let him get hurt and be let down' or curtail his
activities in order to protect him from hurt.

Mothers of adolescent girls have talked to us of a different kind of
risk: pregnancy. A recurring theme throughout this book is how
trusting children with learning disabilities are, and how this worries
their parents, who feel that, if not exactly taboo, the whole area of
contraception and pregnancy is not dealt with openly or adequately
in schools. Boys are also open to sexual risks, of course, as we have
seen above (and see Chapter 9), but parents express additional
worries about their daughters. One mother of a 13-year-old girl told
us:

> 'I know there's all this liberal stuff about the rights of young girls like my
> daughter to have a normal life, including sex. It's all right for social
> workers to go on about it. But she doesn't understand about contra-
> ception and would have to be made to take it and anyway that's no
> answer. And there's no way she could look after a baby'.

There are no easy answers to these complex issues, highlighted in the Law Commission's (1995) report on mental incapacity. A thoughtful discussion is provided by McCarthy (1998) in respect of young women with learning disabilities and sexuality, while Booth & Booth (1994) examine the reality of parenting for both men and women as well as consequences for children (see also Chapter 3). The need to examine the ethical nature of complex interpersonal matters is considered by Warnock (1998), where the question of differing values is discussed.

Conclusion

Children and young people with learning disabilities share the experiences of other marginalised citizens in that they are open to harm and excluded from mainstream activities in the community. On the one hand, they are vulnerable to abuse, neglect or misunderstanding and on the other, incapacity or personal disability are used as reasons why they cannot or should not participate in decisions which concern them. The Law Commission (1995) has usefully addressed these and other issues relating to incapacity, vulnerability and the rights of people with learning disabilities, but its Bill did not get through parliament. Denial of the right to participate in chosen leisure and other activities constitutes a form of abuse in itself (Westcott & Cross, 1996). The child or young person's quality of life suffers, while an awareness of denied opportunities causes individual upset. Such exclusion may then be institutionalised in government policies, as in, for example, the decision to exclude disability from the remit of the Exclusion Unit (see Laura Middleton's letter in *Professional Social Work* (Write Off, 1998)).

Harm to children can be avoided or prevented by recourse to the child protection system although, of course, safety in residential care (or foster care) is by no means guaranteed. Risk assessments, although aiming to protect the child, are not infallible and may sometimes have too narrow a focus. Moreover, protection can have differing goals, and practitioners need to be capable of distinguishing among them in order to clarify their reasons for intervention.

What is certain is that children and young people are themselves very often in risky situations: unable to make their needs fully known, vulnerable to abuse and even subject to chance where professional understanding, agency resources and social work approaches are concerned. The work of professionals in such cases is complex, leading to no easy answers, but to a duty to acquire knowledge of the ways in which disabled children are especially vulnerable and skills in assessment and intervention, to which we shall return in Chapter 11.

Chapter 9

Giving Power to Children and Families

The simple question 'who has power?' arises when we consider the rights of individuals to self-determination in all aspects of their lives. As we have seen, the nature of learning disability often puts others in positions of power, so that the ability to make choices is at best restricted or more probably non-existent. Ethical issues of informed consent and research practices are a part of the equation of power (Stalker, 1999) because the child at the centre may not directly contribute to a decision or discussion that concerns them.

The situation of a child with learning disabilities is greatly removed from that of those with power to influence their lives. First, they are children who in any case (and in many situations properly so) must expect their carers to make decisions on their behalf. Second, as they grow up they often lack communication skills through which to make their needs directly known. Third, although in most cases parents are the best advocates for and protectors of their children, this is not automatically so; and professionals may focus more firmly on parents' needs than on children's, as Welch (1998) succinctly points out.

A hierarchy of knowledge and power usually puts professionals, or experts, at the top, with those who require advice and support on lower levels. Children are placed lower than adults, while children with learning disabilities arguably have the least power. Empowerment is about a process by which people gain control of their lives. The role of professional workers should be to facilitate the process of power, carefully considering the views of children. The aim is to counteract the experience of powerlessness present through membership of a disadvantaged group and to encourage confidence in the ability to conduct one's own life. Social workers should not so much 'empower' others – not a helpful expression, in our view – as enable people to take control of their lives by, for instance, making representations to health, education and welfare services about their need for services, support or advice. People may require initial encouragement, in writing letters, for instance, to express their needs (Fitton, 1994) or in developing the skills of self-help (Adams, 1996).

The situation of children is naturally different from that of adults, although the same issues will arise (see Chapter 2) concerning over- and underprotection of children by parents and carers. Professionals tread a difficult path here. Children with disabilities have special needs, including the need to be understood. It is up to practitioners to develop ways of communicating with children in order to ascertain these needs. If this is not fully taken into account, it is a denial of their right to involvement in matters which directly and ethically concern them.

The need for empowerment

The first question to be asked is why such a need arises in the first place. The medical model of disability demonstrates how a child begins to be disempowered by the very nature of complex profes- sional interactions; and consequent social dependencies, particu- larly in the family, may lead to overprotection of the child, because he or she is seen as vulnerable. This perceived dependency may result in requests for professional involvement. The problem is partly that, in caring for a child with learning disabilities, the responsibilities take their toll of each family member's ability to manage. Cairns (1992) comments on the difficulties which ensue when parents experience sleep disturbance, poor health and physical exhaustion. The consequent professional involvement of social workers and community nurses with parents may eliminate any real sense of self-determination by the children, if there is no concerted effort to involve them as well in discussions and decisions about health, education and other vital concerns. This is usually because many parents need attention in their own right and may be all too ready to allow someone else to take decisions for them, acquiescing to arrangements made on their and their child's behalf for what they believe to be for the best.

If, on the other hand, professional help is seen by carers, especially parents, as putting their child at risk (by, for example, encouraging a son or daughter to be more active in the community, use public transport and so on), then the parents may exercise their protective function by withdrawing permission to participate. Social work practitioners have to enable the persons to make choices while not ignoring parental involvement (Jackson & Jackson, 1999). Thus parental empowerment may be in competition with that of their children and with professional authority, and the sense of partnership which professionals strive to achieve may suffer as a consequence.

In either case, the needs of parents to protect and of professionals to take decisions are often considered at the expense of children's right to be involved. One result will be that communication difficulties and problems with the child's expression of feelings may be cited as reasons for not including the child in planning. Our intent here is to raise awareness of the needs of children and young people whose abilities to express their feelings in words, verbally or by sign language, may be problematic due to difficulties with the use of the more widely used communicative channels. Broadly, our view is that it would be foolish not to recognise that parents speak ably for their children, but it would be equally wrong not to make every effort to communicate in whatever way possible with children themselves.

In 1992, the UK government agreed to be bound by the United Nations Convention on the Rights of the Child (United Nations, 1989). This gives children the right to have a say in matters which affect them. It is also a matter of law: in the UK the Children Act 1989 makes clear that the views of children must be sought over decisions concerning their welfare. The problem for many children with learning disabilities is that they may not be able to express their views in conventional ways; parents generally act as their child's proxy by stating his or her interests as they see them. We ourselves are doing exactly this in our writings and research. The issue which has to be addressed is how all those concerned with the welfare of children can make greater efforts to include them in decision-making.

Beresford (1997) puts forward two arguments against involving children in research: (1) the belief that children cannot be sources of valid data, and (2) that there is a danger of exploiting children. Such objections were earlier countered by Fivush *et al.* (1987), who show that children are capable of reporting matters accurately and that it is adults who misrepresent the data they provide (see also McGurk & Glachan, 1988). It seems to us that such views reflect much more how courts view children's evidence, despite progress in this area. Clearly, what children say about their situation is valid and their perspective vitally important.

The matter of exploitation is more difficult to counter, because present and future vulnerability and long-term damage are harder to quantify or predict. Even here, the issue might be resolved by taking greater care with the research approach adopted in order to minimise any possibility of increasing the child's vulnerability by actively engaging them in research through the medium of trusted others. This may raise the question of contaminated data (whose view is being ascertained, the child's or the interpreter's?) as well as the issue of capacity to give true consent (Law Commission, 1995). Such issues are commonplace to practitioners, who regularly encounter problems in communicating with children with special needs and interpreting their wishes.

In both research and practice, age and developmental factors are also important (see Chapter 3). An adult, for example, has the duty and responsibility not to put a child or young person in a situation in which they cannot make informed decisions; a clear case is that of child sexual abuse, where the child cannot be said to give informed consent and where there is an imbalance of power and status.

In a daily practice context, professionals must be careful in the way that they phrase questions, making a knowledge of child development and language crucial to their work. Sinclair (1996) and Hill (1998) consider how to involve children in decision-making, stressing the need to listen to what they say about services. Although they are writing about children in general, their work has clear relevance for disabled children. Bond (1999) reviews a pack specifically designed for children with learning difficulties to help them communicate their wishes and participate in service design. She stresses, as we do, the necessity for creative and child-friendly tools and environments.

Communication difficulties

Communication difficulties place a major responsibility on carers, first, to understand individual needs, and second, to communicate such needs to people in positions of power. This can be considered as a form of advocacy by unauthorised proxy. Such interpretative views might either misrepresent or enhance the vulnerability and experience of social exclusion for the children concerned (Burke 1998a).

Advocacy through others can bring difficulties, as recognised in recent years by such organisations as Advocacy for Action and well expressed through the publication *We Can Speak for Ourselves*

(Advocacy in Action, 1993). Their work and that of other organisations, such as People First and Changing Perspectives, is having a profound effect on research and service organisations, although not nearly as much as disabled people themselves would like. For example, the powerful letter by (Simone) Aspis (1999), protests at the exploitation by researchers and research institutes of disabled people with learning difficulties.

This puts non-disabled professionals in a difficult position, forcing them to review totally their approach to their work and its dissemination. Many disabled people feel hurt, angry and disempowered at conferences and seminars about them, and understandably so. Nevertheless, it would be difficult to argue that children in general and children with learning disabilities in particular do not need and deserve responsible and concerned adults to help them make their needs and wishes known (Ward, 1998; Ward & Simons, 1998). We firmly believe that it would be an abdication of parental and professional responsibility not to speak up for children.

The rights of non-speaking people and those from ethnic and language minorities to be understood need special acknowledgement. Along with these rights goes the duty of those working in the field of learning disabilities to take every step to learn creative ways of communicating with their clients or patients and assist them as far as possible to communicate directly with influential others, including resource-holders. One of us is a practice teacher, often supervising social work students who undertake placements with people with learning difficulties. One such student, concerned about her lack of ability to communicate with some young people, took the trouble to learn Makaton, which the young people used, as well as becoming computer literate in order to work with them on software programs. Another, with disabilities herself, spent a great deal of time observing the small hand and eye movements of a child with cerebral palsy so that she became able to interpret when he meant 'yes', 'no', ' want a drink', and so on. In this way, she helped him gain control over a fundamental area of his life. She also taught other carers the value of close observation as a key to understanding children.

Both these students remarked that not all the professionals they came across were prepared to take such trouble, placing these apprentices in the position of showing qualified practitioners how they could learn to communicate with disabled children, putting the child first. The case of Neal (Richardson, 1997) is reported in a similar vein to celebrate his achievements in communication, where his body postures were eventually decoded to indicate distress, a simple 'yes' or 'no' to questions asked of him, or other needs to which a response could therefore be made.

Our 1995 research (Burke & Cigno, 1996) and that by Burke (1998c) showed that the needs of children with learning disabilities may easily be overtaken by the wishes of verbally able individuals, usually parents, who articulate these needs for their children. The effect, if not the intent, may be the exclusion of the wishes and feelings of the children themselves. It is worth repeating, though, that parents of children with learning disabilities, like other parents, are most likely to be inextricably bound up in the health and welfare of their children. However, due to the additional stresses of caring, perceptions of their child's needs and wishes might become confused with their own emotional needs.

There are no easy ways to incorporate the views of those whose communicative abilities are not well understood and whose needs are dependent on others. Fitton (1994) provides a detailed account of the carer's responsibilities, but the interpretative quality of the carer's expression of these will often be framed by a need to protect, which itself may deny the rights of the individual. In attempts to unravel the complexities of the interactions which exist between child, carer and professional, the notion of the locus of control offers some clarity.

The locus of control

The *locus of control* (Lefcourt, 1976) is based on principles of social learning theory and therefore can be used in cognitive–behavioural therapy (Burke, 1998c). It provides a framework for the assessment of any situation which requires understanding and some form of action. Burke (1998c) gives examples of its usefulness in the field of children with learning disabilities. Control is seen as either internal or external. Individuals who take responsibility for their own actions and see consequences as a result of their own efforts are said to have an internal locus of control. Those who see situations and outcomes as outside their influence and who believe that their lives are subject to the control of others have an external locus of control.

Understanding the world of the child helps to identify family situations from a child's view, and in so doing aids our determination of reasonable and realistic goals. Children with learning disabilities are often largely dependent on others, and thus have an external locus of control. Behavioural interventions, as well as other kinds, need to recognise this but put into operation a means for redirecting and reinforcing desired behaviours that are within the individual's control. The aim of intervention should be to increase the child's repertoire of skills and choices, enabling a move towards self-determination.

CASE EXAMPLE: **Pauline**

Pauline is a 12-year-old who was diagnosed as being a Down's baby at birth. She is the only child of older parents. Her parents report that they felt that the doctors who were involved dealt with the matter very sensitively. They later found support services useful in alerting them to Pauline's likely needs in the future. At home, neighbours are supportive and will child-sit, but this is partly because of their prior experience with children with learning disabilities; in that respect, the family feel lucky. There are no extended family members available to help; most are elderly and need help themselves, so the family manages alone with some support services when needed. Pauline's mother says that the special needs statement issued by the education authority has caused her some difficulties because she could not understand why it was necessary and what it meant. However, because of the pressures on the family, Pauline now spends one night a week at a hostel attached to the special school she attends. Her parents value what they consider to be much-needed periods of respite care.

While her mother understands Pauline's father's need to be protective ('she is her father's only child'), she is herself unsure whether or not to allow Pauline to do things for herself. This attitude is reflected towards Pauline, who is learning daily living skills at school, but both parents say they are afraid to let her practise these new skills at home. For example, Pauline is not allowed to use the kitchen at home and so on one occasion she crept downstairs in the early hours and cooked her own breakfast. She was told not to do so again because she could burn herself. Pauline is therefore restricted at home and is not encouraged to become more independent. Her parents are aware that they are 'working against' the school but cannot face exposing their daughter to what they see as risky situations.

Comment

Pauline's parents, self-confessedly middle-aged and 'set in our ways', are devoted to her. Like many parents, they coped for years with little professional support; they are used to making decisions for their daughter and getting by with informal help from neighbours. They have only recently been offered, and have begun to take advantage of, professional support.

Some professional advisory input is needed (see Sloper & Turner, 1992) to help empower them actively to seek solutions to problems. Problem-solving needs time and energy, without which families remain suppressed, marginalised and unsupported. Parents are unlikely to provide fully for the needs of their families unless they obtain recognition for themselves and for their roles as carers.

Power and independence

Empowerment results when learning-disabled people have 'control over their lives' (Finklestein, 1993, p. 15). It is not to be confused with independence, although it often includes a political dimension pursued by disability lobbies formed to promote disability rights. The results have achieved recognition such as that represented by the United Nations' (1989) *Declaration of the Rights for Disabled People*. Empowerment also requires a cultural change of view within 'normal' non-learning-disabled society as well as by those who consider themselves disabled. Disability carries its own stigma, often consciously or unconsciously accepted by people with learning disabilities themselves. The learning-disabled individual is a person, not an object of pity due to some tragic circumstance.

Independence, on the other hand, may become synonymous with control of one's own life; it transcends work and daily living to include leisure activities, control and responsibilities in daily decision-making (Lawton, 1993). Gaining control of one's own life is a basic right we all share and, as Oliver (1990) argues, the person who is disabled is the best person to describe what their needs are. Self-empowerment enables that process, as disabled children articulate their needs and, as they grow up, reject well-intentioned, pitying attitudes disguised as caring.

The role of the professional is ambiguous because the task of helping disabled individuals often denies their taking full responsibility for decisions, actions and choices. Parents can be ambivalent towards the professional, uncertain whether the professional is helping too little, causing frustration, or too much, causing them loss of face in managing their affairs. Similarly, the professional can be ambivalent, uncertain about the position of the disabled child in the decision-making forum.

Professional intervention and research on its effectiveness need to clarify the shifting power base which the ambivalent response produces. Professionals' training must therefore include an examination of the need to empower learning-disabled people rather than to discriminate further against them, whether directly by non-communication, or in collusion with parents and others who presume to know what is best for them. If professionals do not act in the best interests of the child, then they may be a potential danger to them, even though such action may be unintended (Burke, 1999). However, to achieve the objective of putting the child first, it is necessary to consider further the role played by informal carers in the empowerment equation.

CASE EXAMPLE: **Jackie**

Jackie is 17 years old, has had optic atrophy from birth and requires medication to control epilepsy. This diagnosis was not confirmed until the age of eight years. She is fully ambulant but has the mental age of a much younger child of about four. Jackie uses imitative speech. She is able to dress and undress herself and generally 'behaves' herself, but needs constant supervision. She is able to feed herself and can do simple household chores like making her own bed. She has a younger half-sister, Helen, aged 12, who understands Jackie's limitations. Her father had difficulty accepting his daughter and, after separating from the family, chose to have little contact with her. Her parents divorced when Jackie was still at pre-school age. Her mother remarried and Helen was born some time later.

Jackie is currently awaiting a place at a special boarding-school, which will care for her until she is 25. At that point she has the prospect of entering some community living scheme with warden support. In the interim, her new school will enable her to develop her social skills. Home leave will be negotiated with her parents in accordance with Jackie's developing needs and wishes.

Comment

This family has encouraged Jackie to become independent; she now has the prospect of living her own life without immediate parental protection on a daily basis. The transition of moving to boarding-school confronted parental expectations because they had always thought Jackie would remain at home. Their plans included a separate flat within the grounds of their own home, from which they could supervise their daughter. Nevertheless, the move to boarding-school is considered a real achievement, welcomed by all. Parents (mother and stepfather) are now beginning to focus on their own needs, together with those of their other daughter.

Each member of the family has been involved in planning for the future and has thus achieved some control over important aspects of their life. In this context, the value of categorising a person by mental age is to be questioned. In Jackie's case, her prospect of leaving home had occurred at a time when most young people would be considering their future needs, whether in employment, at college or university. The difference, however, is that Jackie's parents did not know that a new opportunity might become available, because they had been poorly informed of options and choices. This meant that they had for many years made inappropriate plans, causing unnecessary family distress. Informed choices should be the right of all parents and their children when it comes to such vital issues as living space and education, whether or not the child has a disability.

Conclusion

The role of professionals and lay people alike is to recognise the right of people with disabilities to policies and practice which directly include them. So far, most of the fact-finding and research in this area concerns adults (see, for example, Oliver, 1998). In the case of children, the focus has been mainly on the need for inclusive education policies, as the journal *Inclusion* typifies, although this same journal also covers articles on aspects of human rights and justice for disabled people internationally (Eigher, 1998).

Increased multidisciplinary working is a vital objective for practitioners, who should at least have reached an initial understanding of the meaning of such terms as vulnerability, prevention and social exclusion in the field of disabilities. The examples show that prevention of harm may involve the need to prevent social isolation and counteract vulnerability. Intervention at one level of professional understanding will have an impact on another, and is particularly relevant when monitoring and evaluating inclusive practices.

There is a need to encourage both representation and participation where disabled people are equals. In the case of Pauline, the parents' feelings of responsibility to protect, although well meaning, run the risk of preventing their daughter's steps to a more independent and quality lifestyle. In Jackie's case, her parents had to balance a more objective view of her needs against their own; in the end, they were helped to a decision which enables their daughter to gain a more independent future. The danger is that many disabled children may continue to be excluded in the belief that they are incapable of expressing their own needs and so can be safely ignored. This is clearly a denial of rights from which they need protection.

Chapter 10

Multi-agency Practice

Child care legislation, inquiries, reports and research have given agencies and professionals who work in them important messages about policy and practice with families where there is a child with disabilities (for commentaries on these see, for example, Beresford, 1994; Burke & Cigno, 1996; Cigno with Burke, 1997; Burke & Montgomery, 2000). One such message was contained in the Children Act 1989, with its inclusion of disabled children in section 17 as children 'in need'. The guidance (Department of Health, 1991, 1999) accompanying the Act elaborates on this concept as well as on the necessity for agencies to work together and to support children and their parents through early intervention and partnership. This chapter provides an illustration of how a multi-agency approach might work for children with disabilities.

Family centres were specifically named in the Children Act as a way to support families, since the research on their effectiveness and ability to involve adults and children in the helping process in a non-stigmatising way had already been well documented in the 1980s (Wilmott & Mayne, 1983; De'Ath, 1985; Cigno, 1988). From a health care point of entry, *child development centres* or *teams*, usually operating from a medical base, were also well established in some areas (for a discussion of these, see Hall, 1997).

Education Acts from 1981 pointed to the duty to assess children with special needs, write a statement about these, and provide appropriate schooling. Needs-led assessments and user participation are also key elements of the National Health Service and Community Care Act 1990. A different kind of study from those already mentioned, such as those undertaken by Westcott & Cross (1996) and Russell (1994), has pointed to the vulnerability of children with disabilities to abuse and neglect, both intentional and unintentional, by carers in home and institutional settings; and the need for practitioners to be aware of these issues when carrying out their duties under the Children Act (see Chapter 5 for further discussion of legislation relating to children and families).

In response to these concerns and new duties, many local authorities set up specialised and, to a certain extent in that they involved the health sector, multidisciplinary teams to visit and support families, especially where there is a child with learning difficulties. These efforts were a necessary start to the process of providing good enough services but were not deemed to go far enough in that they fell short of making available a fully coordinated, multi-professional approach. Moreover, a Social Services Inspectorate (1998a) report on services in eight areas found that no authority carried out joint assessments as a matter of routine. In this context, any initiative to involve more than two key agencies in offering a holistic approach to children and carers is bound to represent advances in a coordinated, user-participatory approach to disabled children (McGrath, 1991; Grant, 1992; Appleton *et al.*, 1997; Yerbury, 1997), as we have mentioned elsewhere in this book. New developments need careful evaluation, since the shape of future services may well depend on a mapping of their successes as well as pitfalls, as another government report has made clear (Ball, 1998). The following is an account of how this may be done, through an examination of one such initiative.

Health, Social Services, Education and representatives of the voluntary sector for children with disabilities in one northern region came together to set up a *children's (resource) centre*, one of only a few arising from child development centres or teams, with the object of providing a seamless, multi-agency, pluridisciplinary, 'one-door' approach. From the start, the intention of the service providers was to evaluate this new venture, following the increasingly high policy agenda of obtaining evidence of service effectiveness and user satisfaction. An evaluation of the centre's progress took place approximately two years after its opening (see Cigno & Gore, 1998).

The needs of families

Although, as we know, the needs of children with disabilities and their families are well researched, even over-researched, they are undervalued in terms of due consideration by policy-makers. A constant finding is that families want a coordinated 'keyworker' approach (as advocated in the National Health Service and Community Care Act 1990 and further stressed in the Carers (Recognition and Services) Act 1995), but their experience of service provision is far from this ideal (Anon, 1989; Audit Commission, 1994; Daly, 1998). Carefully coordinated provision that is both imaginative and useful is not much in evidence, despite research findings which have brought disability issues to the public and professional gaze. Dobson & Middleton's (1998) research study reaches the even gloomier conclusion that, in spite of legislation, families have experienced little improvement in services.

The main reasons for this anomaly are:

(1) On the whole, children and individual family units do not, and are not helped to, make their needs known (Burke and Cigno, 1995).
(2) Child protection issues and procedures have taken up the time and resources of most social services departments whose staff has not felt able to concentrate on the interests of children in need (Department of Health, 1995).
(3) Ideologies of economics and power have enabled policy-makers and the public in general largely to ignore disability issues (Corby, 1993; Kennedy, 1995; Oliver, 1998).

The refocusing debate, though (see, for example, Department of Health, 1995; Farmer, 1997), has begun to bring about new and helpful thinking, incorporated once more in an SSI report (Goodinge, 1998).

In many important ways, child happiness or, more mundanely, satisfaction is inextricably linked with that of their main carers. However, the view has been expressed by Oliver & Barnes (1998) as well as by others that recognition of carers' needs may detract from the direct listening to, and focus on, disabled people themselves. The evaluation in question did therefore try to assess children's satisfaction directly as well as through key others.

The multi-agency approach

A smooth, integrated approach implies that access to information and services are readily available, preferably at one point of entry, where traditional service divisions disappear. Failure to provide this results in having to 'tell your story' over and over to different professionals on the one hand, and experiencing gaps in services on the other (Baldwin & Carlisle, 1994). At the same time, parents expect professionals to have specialised knowledge about disability and services (see Chapter 5).

Three decades ago, the Social Services Act 1970 was passed in an attempt to bring together services previously administered independently. Education welfare services were, however, excluded from the Act; and the health services continued to operate under a national umbrella as well as with different geographical boundaries and structures from those of local authorities. This is still the case, although the government's White Paper *Modernising Social Services* (Department of Health, 1998) is determined that these barriers will be removed in order to improve services (see also the news article by White, 1998).

Paradoxically, the trend within social services departments is once more towards specialisation and division, with services for adults divided from services for children and families (and sometimes subdivisions within children's services), while at the same time many services are becoming less local and therefore less accessible to the public. Yet the situation is complex, for some specialist teams – for example, community mental health teams – are multidisciplinary. What all this indicates is that no structure is permanent, and this could work to the advantage of people needing services if their needs, not those of the professionals, prevail.

This last condition is key. The reasons why various professionals find it difficult to work together have been well rehearsed: each discipline has a different and separate education and training of varying lengths; their focus and status differ; allegiance is to separate and often powerful validating and professional bodies (Etzioni, 1969; Ackoff, 1985; Hugman, 1991). Moreover, professionals often work in different organisations, public, voluntary, private or not-for-profit, each with its own internal hierarchy and divisions of labour (Reason, 1994; Wistow, 1994; Jones & Joss, 1995). Some, like medical practitioners, have a long tradition and powerful identity while others, like social workers, are relatively new on the scene and possess a less clear and not wholly positive identity. The aim of any attempt to provide a one-door, multi-agency service must be to subsume these known factors under the common aim of providing the best possible service to children and their families. We now go on to examine the strategy for testing how far the objectives of the multi-agency children's centre under scrutiny were being reached.

Methodology

Full details of the methodology are given in Cigno & Gore (1998). A multi-method approach was used to increase the validity of the research by providing a view of the area under study from different angles using different sources. Non-participant observation took place of:

- general activity within the building
- children in classroom and therapy/play sessions
- various staff management and team meetings
- specific groups like the siblings group and the after-school group.

Semi-structured interviews and focus groups were used to gain a picture of the views and experiences of centre staff, senior personnel from participating agencies and persons from other agencies with a professional interest in the centre. A brief survey questionnaire was sent out to parents, followed by interviews with a small number of these. Documentation sources were also used to help verify some of the data acquired from respondents.

Sample populations

Overall, 51 members of staff (four voluntary workers, the rest practitioners or administrators) took part. All teams working within the building were represented: multi-agency team (all disciplines), administration, child development services (nurses and therapists), Barnardos children's disability team (social workers), educational services (teachers, Portage and support workers), community learning disability team (community nurses, psychologists and occupational therapists) and the medical team (paediatricians and other specialists).

Eighty-four parents out of a possible 165 (according to the centre's database) were involved in the study. Seventy-five of these were recent or current centre users; five of these were subsequently interviewed (see below for selection criteria and response). The remaining nine were members of parent-led groups using the centre and its resources.

A total of 62 children were observed. Forty-seven were children with a wide range of special needs (of these, four were able to provide some comments about the centre). The remaining 15 were their brothers and sisters.

Staff from key organisations concerned with children with physical and learning disabilities operating locally, the local community health councils and social services department's area teams were also consulted. Care was taken not to exclude the views of any relevant person or group. Lastly, the views of groups using the centre as a venue for meetings (for example, health education training) were sought in a more ad hoc fashion.

As this study was concerned with looking at a multi-agency service, we selected for interview professionals from all levels and all agencies operating within the centre. Meetings which reflected both multi-agency working in practice and the efforts made to enhance parent partnership through inclusion in the centre's various committees and groups were observed. No one refused to take part. Individual confidentiality was assured to all.

The views of families who had used the centre in the last six months were sought in order to ensure that opinions expressed were as relevant to current service provision as possible. We also spoke informally (always with the parents' consent) to a small number of children (see the useful article by Roberts & Wellard (1997) on the ethics of including children in research projects). In the main, child satisfaction was measured in three ways: by obtaining the carer's perception; through observing children's demeanour and behaviour when entering the reception area and while participating in structured and unstructured events; and through a child's incidental feedback to us when we were in the centre.

A total of 156 questionnaires went out to parents resulting in 75 responses, a high response rate to a postal questionnaire, particularly from an imperfect database. The knowledge that the research was carried out by an independent institution was probably important in obtaining a reasonable response, as well as the use of a short questionnaire asking only basic questions about family size and type, services used and likes and dislikes about the centre. Overburdening this vulnerable population, who have little time in their busy and often stressful lives to fill in forms, is a form of oppressive practice of which researchers and others need to be well aware. Nevertheless, of those who did reply, almost all expressed their willingness to be interviewed at a later stage. As the overwhelming majority expressed rather fulsomely satisfaction with the centre, and time was limited, we deliberately chose for follow-up the one dissatisfied family, two of the ten partly satisfied, with 3 of the 64 who declared themselves wholly satisfied.

Family characteristics and use of services

Eighty-four per cent of those who took part in the survey were the birth mothers, 11% the birth fathers and 5% foster carers. Most children with disabilities had at least one sibling, while the average age of the disabled child was three. Over two-thirds of the families still attended the centre; the rest were recent users.

Broadly, the three main services with established bases in the centre were health, education and social work support, the latter delegated to Barnardos by the social services department. Many families in fact used more than one agency, and some aspects of all three main services, but systematic data about individual patterns of use were not available. The overlap in use is shown by the fact that three-quarters of the children were patients of the health services (and were likely to be seen by both specialist doctors and nurses), half received help from education staff and one-third were supported, together with their families, by the social work team.

In addition, approximately one-quarter had been through the children's centre assessment, a multi-agency procedure. Thus our sample consisted of families who had used a wide variety of services. Systematic data on the type of disability present in our child population were not available, although we found that a wide range of disability was represented, including speech and language difficulties, learning disabilities, behavioural problems, cerebral palsy, Down's syndrome and autism.

There were two measures of success and satisfaction: (1) the views, and our observations, of families using the centre; (2) the views, and our observations, of professionals working within and outside the centre. The two main concerns were how far centre staff had achieved multi-agency and pluridisciplinary working and were meeting the needs of families.

Multi-agency, pluridisciplinary working

Parents' views

A considerable number of parents said that what they liked most about the Centre was that services were 'under one roof' and appeared seamless. Some parents referred to the fact that they had used services, such as the child development centre, prior to the children's centre's opening and felt that the new centre was a 'massive improvement' in terms of integration and centralisation of services. This was supported by our (limited) interview data. Many parents made particular reference to the fact that if they needed another service within the centre then they would be referred on accordingly, often via one 'key worker'. They only needed to go 'down the corridor' to be in touch with another practitioner, usually on the same day, thus avoiding multiple journeys and wearisome explanations. Parents' typical comments were:

'The total care of the child is addressed by the various specialists in the one centre.'

'Going to one place is less daunting for me and my child.'

'Every service is here, so if one person doesn't know something they can put you through to someone else.'

'Before, you had to take your child to the clinic and wait months for tests and you didn't know who to ring if you hadn't been given an appointment. With the children's centre, you ring one place and it's central for all the appointments needed.'

Staff views

Most of the staff interviewed and observed demonstrated a strong commitment to multi-agency working; and, like the families, almost all had previously experienced fragmented service provision. We asked the different managers for their views of the multi-agency approach and they all responded in a similar vein:

'It's essential . . . Children's needs are complex and don't fit into neat little boxes'

(head of educational services).

'It's an excellent philosophy . . . Because of the nature of disability, there are a lot of people involved in the care of the child and so working together is important'

(manager of child development services team).

'Families see so many different people, they often can't differentiate between them, so it helps by having us all here'

(manager of Barnardos team).

'It's vital, as they [families] want to know that they've got one person to go to who is looking after all their interests'

(manager of community learning disability team).

The work undertaken by the multi-agency coordinator included attempts to bring together the services and staff, resolving any difficulties as they arose: a complex and difficult task, crucial to the centre's aims. In our interviews and focus groups, managers, practitioners and administrative staff were asked how well they felt the various agencies were integrated and to give reasons for their answer. They were given three possible answers to choose from: 'well integrated'; 'fairly integrated'; 'poorly integrated'. The most frequent response was 'fairly integrated'. The comments explaining their response reflected the difficulties in achieving integration and the high standards staff set themselves for success. This contrasts with the overwhelming satisfaction expressed by parents with regard to multi-agency collaboration.

Many of the positive comments made by those working in or with the centre were about the day-to-day informal integration and communication among agencies and professionals, particularly with regard to direct work with children and the handling of referrals. Several respondents said that communication among services was 'much easier' and 'more natural' than before the centre existed, due to the fact that these services were now housed together. In general, centre staff felt that they could 'knock on doors' to approach professionals from other disciplines or agencies as problems arose, rather than waiting for correspondence and telephone calls. Many felt that this 'instant access' to different professionals helped to make the work carried out on behalf of a family much more efficient.

But comments along the lines of 'there's too much bureaucracy' highlight what for many staff is a problem in multi-agency working: liaising on a formal level. This could account for another theme which emerged from the data: a staff-perceived risk of lack of common purpose in the centre, despite general enthusiasm for the centre's philosophy of working together. As one manager succinctly put it, 'people do not seem to have a grasp of the whole'.

Although staff responded and linked up on an informal basis, many saw formal meetings as a time-consuming extra and they were therefore not taken seriously. This is partly explained by, in the words of one manager, 'the differing backgrounds of the various personnel in the centre'. The agencies might use very different models of child care (for example, a 'social' versus 'medical' model). This could lead to conflicts between one team and another and to 'some treading on toes' during management meetings, where attempts to work together could cause confusion over who should be doing what. The multi-agency administrator commented that, as all managers have equal status, it is hard to prioritise one aspect of services over another, or assign certain issues to a specific manager.

Data from our focus groups support these findings. Attendance at multi-professional staff meetings was fluid. Elaborating on this, many practitioners from all the agencies stressed that, due to the commitment they had to their own teams and their heavy work-loads, they 'integrate' with other agencies only as far as they need to. Again, this relates to the development of an informal, ad hoc nature of communication among teams, dictated by issues surrounding particular child cases and practice. And as a senior medical practitioner commented, 'without a centralised database, it is difficult to see the whole of what is happening to a child'.

Despite reservations, all the team members we spoke to were open to 'creative solutions' and expressed a strong willingness to improve their level of formal collaboration, including work on a computerised database. Measures had recently been put in place to improve joint working – for example, multi-agency assessment procedures and the setting up of management groups. In addition, certain teams had held seminars which were designed to promote understanding of their practices for other teams.

External views

Most of the statutory and voluntary organisations valued the work of the centre. Parent-led groups were highly satisfied with the centre as a base for their meetings and with staff support. A few expressed some dissatisfaction. Three linked issues were raised:

- liaison with health services in the rural catchment area
- some inconsistency in a child's care plan due to the involvement of two community health trusts
- lack of information regarding the availability of certain services outside the centre.

Meeting the needs of families

Parent/carer satisfaction

Parents were asked to state whether they were satisfied with the centre and its services and to give reasons for their answer. The vast majority of parents were satisfied with the centre and could articulate why. Many, naturally enough, compared their present satisfaction with past frustrations over fragmented services. Nearly one-third commented that the building was 'child-friendly'. Almost one-quarter made direct reference to the children's play area, stating that this was a big attraction for their children. As one parent commented:

'Whenever I mentioned the children's centre, he would say, 'Oh, can I play on the fire engine?' He was very happy to go because of that.'

An important element of satisfaction for families was the short waiting time for appointments. This enabled them to see more than one professional in the same day; and those who had other arrangements (for example, the school run) were able to keep to them.

Nearly two-thirds of parents gave the impression that they viewed the children's centre as being like a 'home from home'. The most common words used to describe staff and the atmosphere of the centre were 'friendly', 'helpful', 'understanding', 'relaxed', 'welcoming' and 'informal'. Some parents made direct reference to the 'parents' room' (a large, bright, comfortable room with a kitchen corner) and the fact that this enabled them to meet others, share experiences and wait for their children in a warm and friendly environment. Overall, parents felt that the centre and its good staff–parent relations meant that their lives were made much easier, with the help they received tailored to their individual needs and circumstances. The following parent statements exemplify this:

'It is much handier going to the centre, especially when you're doing two different sessions in one day – you can cook dinner in the parents' room in between!'

'When attending the children's centre we felt part of something, where everyone was doing their best for our child and we could openly discuss anything ... and we made good friendships with other parents in a relaxed atmosphere. You felt at home there.'

A major aim of the centre is to promote parent partnership: a parents' advisory group was instrumental in ensuring that parent representatives were included in the management groups. As already mentioned, many parent-led groups used the centre as a venue for meetings. Although the philosophy of empowering parents to play an active role in the care and assessment of their children was being put into practice, both staff and parents acknowledged the continuing need to encourage parent participation. Many parents are not used to making decisions alongside professionals, whose task is therefore to increase their confidence to do so.

Most parents indicated that there was nothing they disliked about the centre. The reasons why some parents were only partly satisfied and one was dissatisfied tended to be idiosyncratic and not indicative of any trend. Typically, the less than completely satisfied carers thought that their children had not received enough of a particular service.

The problem of transition from the centre to mainstream or special school was an important area which some parents felt to be inadequately addressed by the centre's services. Transitions are known to be a time of particular stress for families with a disabled child (see Chapter 7). Even wholly satisfied parents said that they would like more support when their child had to move to school. As one of the parents interviewed said:

> 'It [the children's centre] lets you down when you have to make the transition from there to normal school: you get all this help and then nothing! Nobody understands or knows your child [when starting school], so you feel you're starting from scratch.'

A few parents thought that the centre did not impart information about available external services, such as other support and play facilities, and this meant that they might miss out at times of need.

Child satisfaction

Children were observed in various activities and situations. Staff used formal criteria and procedures regularly during classroom and therapy sessions to monitor progress and changes in the child's behaviour. All these activities and sessions took place in safe and child-friendly surroundings. Lengthy observations led us to the conclusion that children were in an environment appropriate to their needs, felt at ease in the centre, and benefited from the attention they received. These conclusions were very similar to parents' opinions of benefits to their child.

We were also able to speak briefly with some of the children of the parents we interviewed. The following comments were typical:

> 'I like the doctor. He's kind to me.'

> 'I thought it was really good as they had big tunnels [in the play area].'

> 'Everyone is really funny.'

> 'I like playing on the fire engine.'

Staff views

Practitioners, managers and other staff were asked how far they felt the children's centre met the needs of parents, children and siblings.

There were three possible answers: 'meets their needs'; 'partly meets their needs'; and 'fails to meet their needs'. Most staff thought that the centre met parents' and disabled children's needs, but only partly met the needs of siblings.

The general consensus was that, as most of the services a family might need were in one place, parents and children could access these services quickly and appropriately. Some argued that, before the centre existed, families may have had to wait a long time for services, may not have been aware of certain services, and/or had received inappropriate care. Staff presented as being committed to receiving children and their families in a friendly and non-stigmatising fashion, assessing their needs before delivering care in partnership with them.

Staff recognised the need for more services for brothers and sisters in order to better meet the needs of the whole family (see Chapter 6). Another area for improvement highlighted was the need to reach out to families who did not live within the urban radius of the centre. In an earlier study, Ross (1990) also identified this weakness in a multi-agency centre approach to children with disabilities, while Singer (1996) suggests that, in providing so much, such centres may deplete local support networks: an insubstantial argument, in our view.

Overall assessment

To sum up, the main points of the evaluation of the children's centre are:

- The vast majority of parents were satisfied with the centre; they appreciated that services were 'under one roof' and, in comparison with previous services, a more efficient and holistic service was provided.

- Most of the needs of families appeared to be met by the centre; in particular, children appeared at ease in a child-friendly environment.

- Parent partnership is a central aim of the centre and is well on its way to being realised.

- Some parents felt that improvement in certain areas is still required: more help for families during the transitionary period when children move from the centre into mainstream schools; and more information regarding outside services.

- Views of professionals regarding multi-agency working con-trasted with those of parents. Staff thought that while they worked well on an informal level and were committed to the multi-agency approach, more common purpose was needed to provide an integrated service on a formal and strategic level.

- Accessibility to the centre for families living in rural areas is poor compared with those living more locally: an obvious point, but one which needs to be addressed.

- A complete and accessible database is essential to enable agencies to provide a holistic care plan for families.

Parents and carers have consistently repeated that they want a coordinated, 'one door' approach to their child and that matters like time spent on appointments, surroundings, and knowledgeable and welcoming practitioners are important to them. This study of one attempt to put these principles into practice reinforces the view that, while obstacles remain, a multi-agency centre approach is the right way forward to the provision of services in partnership with families and, despite the question asked by Hudson (1995), is attainable.

Reflections on multi-agency practice

We pondered why there were differences between the cautious perceptions of professionals of their efforts and the positive experiences reported by families. One possible explanation is that parents are modest in their expectations, or fearful that, if they complain, they might have a service withdrawn. This did not appear to be the case, since not only did parents talk freely to us about services and staff – and offer specific criticism at times – but our findings were based on extensive observations of children and parents in the centre and at meetings where we used objective cri-teria of assessing behaviour indicative of pleasure and satisfaction.

Another, and perhaps more plausible, reason might be that most of the families compared the centre's set-up with past experiences of trying to access services at different points of entry and in uncon-genial surroundings. This underlines the desirability and success of a multi-agency approach. Carers and children did not perceive the tensions and difficulties reported by staff, a strong measure of the professionals' success in working in a child- and family-centred way, not allowing professional differences and deficiences to show.

Multi-agency centres may never be completely trouble-free, in the same way as any service strives for, rather than reaches, perfection. One area of discontent expressed by some professionals was that families in more rural parts did not benefit from services because of difficulty of access and different agency and professional boundaries. Multi-agency centres, where they exist, tend to be situated in large, urban areas; rural and small-town populations therefore may miss out although, in theory, they are entitled to use the services. This is a serious and long-standing issue for service delivery in general. Strategies are needed for either bringing people to central services or, more appropriately, bringing a multi-agency approach to a wider geographical area and a more scattered population. In this connection, an up-to-date database is essential for identifying and locating need in the community as a tool for service planning.

Putting structures like joint meetings and committees for multi-disciplinary working into place does not mean that they will work. It would be naive to think that practitioners from different backgrounds, even within the same organisation, will ever be in total accord. Nevertheless, professionals on all levels must be willing to play an active role in the general running of a multi-agency centre in order to present as one service. At the same time, diversity and choice should be respected and even deemed an essential part of a service which attempts to meet all the varying needs of the family. Each team could follow the example of other teams by presenting periodic seminars aimed at enhancing mutual understanding among agencies and providing a basis on which 'creative solutions' could be established. Above all, having a multi-agency coordinator is essential.

The advantages of a multi-agency approach far outweigh the drawbacks. The current interest in 'one-stop' resource centres for children with disabilities is fortunately likely to continue, particularly now there is evidence that policymakers are listening to what families have been saying for years, resulting in government endorsement through the White Paper (Department of Health, 1998) of a truly seamless service.

Acknowledgement

The research article by K. Cigno and J. Gore, 'A seamless service: meeting the needs of children with disabilities through a multi-agency approach', on which this chapter is based, first appeared in *Child and Family Social Work*, published by Blackwell Science, 1999.

Chapter 11

Promoting Positive Practice

The previous chapters have concentrated on extending knowledge of the experience of learning disability from the family's point of view, with indications of lessons for practice. In this chapter, we consider further professional involvement with family members as an inclusive approach, where individual needs will be identified and met; and where the image of families' uncertainty about future needs, if not entirely removed, is at least reduced. The emphasis on valuing the child's and family's role in assessment of appropriate services increases rather than decreases the importance of the professional's part in the process. Assessing the optimum level of input is not easy, but we have found that many families are far from reticent about expressing their needs; and often what is required is a practitioner who listens carefully, involves the family in assessment and is then prepared to act on the information accumulated. The initial aim is to convey warmth, genuineness and empathy in the helping relationship in order to avoid making hasty decisions, based on poor information, little analysis, and with little understanding of the consequences.

Positive practice

We have been keen to promote a model of practice based on an integration of the medical and social models, transforming this into an approach capable of recognising both kinds of needs which have an impact on day-to-day life (see Chapter 1). The arguments for this integrated model take into account the need to eliminate oppressive practices and to promote positive images of disability. Thus practice is designed to make choice a realistic option for families and their children. In developing this approach, we emphasise the overlap between medical and social aspects of service provision, although this view is by no means universally accepted (see, for example, Gault, 1999). Even the 'feel-good' term *integration* can be misunderstood; as used by Allen (1998), it could mean something which is done to people with disabilities, as in compulsory assimilation. A better, though not synonymous, term is *inclusion*, because the latter word conveys the idea of holism as a driving principle of policy, ensuring a mutually agreed process among all those involved.

In defining disability, the tendency in the past was to consider the person categorised first by the form of the disability. This led to seeing not the person but rather the disability (Dalrymple & Burke, 1995). Anti-oppressive practice should be about the need to understand people's needs, actively seeking their understanding of matters which affect their lives. One result may be a struggle to resolve, or choose between, conflicting opinions on vital issues, plus an increasing recourse to the law to resolve them, as two recent cases have shown. Where severe intellectual and communicative impairment is the case, this may mean that the courts have to decide three things: (1) what the person him- or herself would want; (2) the weight carried by the wishes and intentions of those closely involved, usually the parent; and (3) the wider implications for others, present and future, who may be in a similar position.

The law itself often allows room for interpretation. In the case – the first of its kind – of the mother seeking permission for her 'fairly' severely learning-disabled 27-year-old son to have a vasectomy against a future possibility of his fathering a child, the court overrode her wishes on the grounds that it was an unnecessary invasion of his person for the purpose of preventing a hypothetical future event. The verdict was that this did not warrant medical intervention (Dyer, 1999). However, in another case where the mother did not want doctors to remove artificial life support from her adult son, whose wishes were also unknown, the court ruled that the hospital was right not to accede to her wishes and did not act illegally, as she had alleged (Valios, 1999).

Either judgment is not without controversy. In the latter case, Lord Woolf in the Appeal Court said, somewhat paradoxically, that courts must resolve matters if there was 'grave conflict' between parents and medical staff, but for the court to 'try ... to produce clarity where, alas, there is no clarity at the moment is in my judgement an inappropriate task for the courts' (Valios, 1999, p. 12). Meanwhile, the government's 1995 Green Paper *Who Decides?* on these and other mental health and impairment issues still remains a consultation document, although, as we write, a White Paper is expected.

The Law Commission's report on mental incapacity (Law Commission, 1995), which just preceded the Green Paper, was laid before parliament but was not passed: a loss to the public, in our view. It contains, among other things, extremely useful definitions of vulnerability, harm, exploitation and the 'objecting client' (p. 160, paragraph 9.10), going on to say, 'By making this clear, we intended to strike the necessary balance between the need to protect people with disabilities or frailties and the need to respect autonomy' (p. 161, paragraph 9.10). The Law Commission's remit was all vulnerable adults of 16 and over 'if by reason of old age, infirmity or disability (including mental disorder within the meaning of the Mental Health Act 1983) he is unable to take care of himself or to protect himself from others' (p. 158, paragraph 9.5). Thus the report is clearly relevant to the two cases mentioned above and to those of other young people described in these pages.

If the needs of those we define as children are considered potentially different from the expressed view of parents, the holistic model of social work, which *ipso facto* is based on social aspects of child disabilities while taking into account the perspectives of other disciplines, has further room for conflict. The generational divide is also a factor.

In the legal cases quoted above, the judgments were concerned not with what is right or wrong, but rather with attempting to understand the complexities of life, with its varying difficulties, conflicts and misunderstandings. A social work assessment should not necessarily be expected to make judgements with which the courts themselves feel ill-equipped to deal. Social workers can help to reflect and represent the varied elements of people's lives and help families clarify for themselves alternative courses of action with their possible consequences. Solutions are not always neat, clear-cut and logically formed, but reflect individual, family and societal needs.

Such matters are never easy to accommodate for the professional eager for a successful outcome, where everyone is satisfied. Case recordings, an important part of practice, should accurately reflect summaries of wants and needs, together with expressed uncertainties. Over time, some of these unknowns may be resolved and some solutions to problems found, hence the need for regular reviews, with full collaboration of all those concerned. The need for positive practice is essentially driven by a belief in people's strengths, which should also be recorded, a point to which we return later in this chapter.

A situation of serious individual need will always outweigh the refusal of a family to allow access to one of its members who is thought to be suffering, a matter also considered by the Law Commission. The clear but unhappy illustration of this is that, when one family member physically or sexually abuses another, the victim's needs prevail over those of the abuser. The immediate need for protection of the victim is the primary consideration. Unless there are particular family circumstances warranting the removal of the child, the perpetrator should leave the home. In some cases, this may mean overriding a child's wishes as well as those of the non-abusing carer. In other words, we place the needs of the child first. The important consideration here is that social work has a dual, conflicting aim: preventing abuse and maintaining family cohesion. We have already identified how families who require social work intervention function along a continuum of powerless to powerful; and experience varying degrees of inclusion or exclusion (Fig. 1.1, p. 4).

The use of respite care

Stress factors may be identified by an assessment of the ability of the family to function across a range of areas. Hill's (1958) ABC-X model of family stress indicates how a family might cease to function adequately as states of stress increase to the point of crisis. This increase, as is shown in Hopson's (1981) identification of stages of stress, promotes crisis reactions and clearly points to the need for preventive strategies designed to maintain family function and to avoid a breakdown in family care.

A child's admission to the care (looked after) system might remove temporary strain and crisis in the family unit but would only be considered as a last resort. To the child, this course of action may appear punitive, aimed at punishing him or her for wrongdoing. This is one reason why many parents initially do not wish to consider respite care: they feel guilty at wanting it and are afraid of the child's distress. This is true particularly when their child is young (see the example of Joe below). Some parents of young children told us that they might consider respite care 'later'. Once parents had used respite facilities, they were unequivocal in their praise, afterwards feeling that they could not survive without them (Burke & Cigno, 1996).

Arguably, respite care benefits the carers and possibly other family members more than the child receiving it. This is an important point to consider, especially when the children in question are unable to express their opinion. Parents maintain that they would not allow their child to go away unless he or she were happy about it; and we did come across one or two instances where families had refused to continue using respite care 'because he wasn't happy'. The use of respite care is perhaps a case where (if we assume that some children, at least, do not welcome but put up with it) the greater good takes precedence over the individual good; but it is also indicative of a realistic acceptance that some parents could not continue to care for their disabled child, year after year, without respite. Planned respite from caring can increase the overall quality of care within the family (see Burke 1991).

One parent expressed the benefits of short periods of respite care in the following words:

> 'I only fully realised how much I loved Matthew when he was away from home – then I could rest, so when he returned I welcomed him with open arms. I didn't want him to ever leave me, but it's for the best. I'm no good to him worn out, tired, exhausted, resenting the attention he needed when I could give myself none'
>
> (mother of 13-year-old Matthew).

According to the parents in our 1995 study (Burke & Cigno, 1996), one of the greatest advantages of respite care was its flexibility. It appeared to be one of the few resources geared to respond to different family need and rhythm, although this was less true for respite foster care. The school hostel, for example, could accommodate children variably on a weekday, at weekends, on alternate weekends and in emergencies. Our conclusion is that respite care is a key service for families and contributes a great deal to the well-being of families as an entity and to the alleviation of stress.

Multi-use of formal and informal support

Some families successfully use both formal and informal sources of support (see Chapters 4 and 5). What they lack, in most cases (multi-agency centre users are the exception), is a sense of how services fit together; support is good, but there is no linking element. We noted in Chapter 10 how important this was to families who had experienced a 'one door' approach to support for their children.

The following case illustrates how a family uses support services well, but has not yet achieved a sense of direction. Rather, it remains apparently happily dependent on a high level of service provision and social networks.

CASE EXAMPLE: Joe

Joe, aged five, lives with both parents, his nine-year-old brother and two-year-old sister in a large, terraced house in a northern city. The home is welcoming, with toys much in evidence, as is a large friendly dog, given to enthusiastic welcoming displays when visitors call.

Joe's family was helped by the Portage service during his pre-school years. This made the transition to special school less traumatic for him, and provided a necessary stage in his social and educational development, enabling him and his parents to be prepared for his move into an infants reception class. During this period, mother took Joe to the child development centre where she received considerable guidance on the type and availability of services which might be helpful to the family. Joe's diagnosis, 'autistic tendencies' (mentioned in Chapter 1), followed uncertainties about whether he was, in fact, deaf, a fear the family raised when he was only one year old. His learning disability was suspected at this stage but was only confirmed after further testing the following year. At five, Joe no longer needs nappies since he is continent day and night.

Joe has poor speech and, probably as a consequence of his verbal limitations, makes known his needs by a great deal of vigorous activity, gesturing to convey his wishes in a variety of ways. He is making progress at learning Makaton sign language at school, and is now able to say 'thank you' and 'more', but this is still insufficient to compensate for age-appropriate verbal communication. Joe enjoys being with his brother and sister, gaining much pleasure, too, from playing with the family pet dog.

Family support is provided by maternal grandparents and by talking with other parents and friends. The children get on well together, although Joe's mother finds time spent with her older son helps her preserve a sense of normality.

Service involvement includes speech therapy, which is highly valued, and is cited as the cause of Joe's improving, though limited, verbal ability. Educational psychology provided early help with Joe's feeding habits, while social work input resulted in an approach to the Family Fund and a successful application for a grant for a washing machine. However, although service input and informal help have made a difference to the family, the parents still feel that support arrived in a rather haphazard fashion, uncoordinated, from a variety of sources.

The future is not contemplated too deeply. The hostel at school has yet to be used, neither parent being sure whether they wish to make use of it or not, particularly as Joe is still only five and in the early stages of his formal education. Joe's diagnosis is still somewhat tentative, despite having received a statement of special needs, and so this area remains something of a question mark for the family. The parents do not worry about this:

> 'Joe is Joe, a different label is not going to make him suddenly think he is someone else.'

The current level of family and friendship support, plus an increasing use of the sitter service made available by the social services department, combined with financial help from a national charity for the new washing machine, maintain the quality of family life at a reasonable level. Social activities are well organised. The expectation for Joe's future is that he will gain more specialist help as and when it is needed.

Comment

Joe's family helps illustrate the early benefits from the Portage service and from attending a child development centre. This positive start has formed their attitudes towards professional services. The tentative diagnosis of Joe's condition has yet to make an impact on the family. However, while visits to the child development centre have helped access to useful information concerning support to meet Joe's needs, the fact remains that a keyworker was not available to coordinate a general overview of these needs, although all the different specialists with whom the parents had or have contact are doing a good job. A single, knowledgeable resource person is needed if the positives gained from professional involvement are to be optimised.

Other uncertainties also exist, particularly regarding the use of respite care and Joe's future needs, but the overwhelming picture is positive, since Joe's parents feel confident that help will be at hand when they need it. Joe has already managed one transition (from home to infant school) well. He is well integrated in his family, who in turn are part of a wider family and community. With continuity of help, the likelihood is that he and his family will make progress.

Our intent is to promote positive practice by recognising the needs of the child with learning disabilities within the family context. However, while we think that such a general approach will encourage families towards a sense of empowerment in making choices, determining their own needs and helping their child to do likewise, at times families need psychosocial intervention to help with specific issues such as a child's skill development and, on occasion, problem behaviours.

Social learning theory and helping approaches

It is important for practitioners to recognise that, within an approach aimed at advocating environmental and attitudinal change and organising resources, listening to parents often reveals that day-to-day strategies in the here and now can improve child–parent interaction and enhance the quality of life for the whole family. We have seen how Portage, firmly based on a 'no-fail', step-by-step approach to a child's learning in the home, is enthusiastically received by parents. It is an example of how parents want clear advice and tried-and-tested methods which they can learn to use themselves to help their child. One of the areas where parents in our 1995 survey were not getting help was that of behaviour problems: mealtimes, bedtimes, shouting and hitting were especially mentioned (Burke & Cigno, 1996). Social learning theory (SLT) offers a clear framework for helping children with behaviour problems which, as many parents told us, can lead them to exhaustion and desperation.

Sutton's (1994) definition of (SLT) is clear and useful:

'Social learning theory comprises a large body of concepts which, happily, are recognised by researchers in the disciplines of both psychology and sociology. It concerns how children and adults learn patterns of behaviour, as a result of social interaction, or simply through coping with the environment ... it suggests how to focus upon the practical rather than the pathological, upon people's strengths and potentials rather than upon their weaknesses or shortcomings, and upon how to empower those with whom we work'

(pp. 5–6).

Within this approach, Sutton & Herbert's (1992; see Sutton, 1994) ASPIRE framework for intervention provides a thorough guide.

This fits well with our integrated model of practice (see Fig. 1.2 p. 9). Briefly, the acronym identifies the five stages to working with individuals and families on specific problems (after Sutton, 1994, pp. 8–9):

(1) **AS** – Assessment: focus on the
    (1) What? question – what problems, needs, etc.
    (2) Which? problems, etc., need priority attention
    (3) Who? are the key people involved
    (4) Why? have the problems, etc., arisen (try to obtain a shared understanding)

(2) **P** – Planning: focus on the
    (5) How? question – how are we together going to address the problems, etc. Identify shared objectives
    (6) Negotiate a shared plan (may be written down)

(3) **I** – Implementation: focus on
    (7) Putting the plan into action

(4) **RE** – Review: focus on
    (8) Reviewing and monitoring how the plan is working
    (9) Evaluating the effectiveness of the plan
        How far have the objectives been achieved?
        Do we need to make a new assessment?

Families and practitioners find this model useful (one of us uses it in practice and teaches it to students); it has been employed successfully with a variety of families. Within the assessment stage, behaviour problems, for instance, can be closely described by answering the four 'W' questions, enabling an identification of the *antecedents* (where does the behaviour take place? who is there? etc.), the *behaviour* itself (what exactly does the child do?) and its *consequences* (what happens next? what maintains the behaviour?).

Cognitive–behavioural therapy recognises that the behaviour of one human being is influenced by and influences the behaviour of another; and both influence and are influenced by other aspects of their environment as well as by thoughts surrounding the behaviour in question. Behaviours are maintained because there is some kind of pay-off, even though this pay-off may not always be obvious.

The desirability of exploring behavioural approaches in relation to children with severe levels of learning disabilities is sometimes, but not inevitably, more difficult because of the child's conceptual and intellectual problems in identifying a link between cause-and-effect experiences. Where an association is difficult to make, then traditionally rewarding or, more correctly, reinforcing mechanisms are less likely to be meaningful. For example, the child who likes food but does not or cannot associate eating with mealtimes, will need help to learn that he or she should sit at the table in order to receive food. It may take longer for such a child to learn that there are links between sitting at the table, eating and feeling pleasantly full and satisfied. Through calm and consistent routines, particularly with the assistance and example of other children, the child and family can be helped to experience mealtimes as pleasurable occasions instead of a battleground.

Regaining control

We mentioned the locus of control in Chapter 9, suggesting that control (see Burke, 1998c; Burke 1999, for a detailed discussion) is seen as either internal or external. Individuals who take responsibility for their own actions and see reinforcement and change as a consequence of their own efforts are said to have an internal locus of control. Those who see situations and outcomes as outside their influence and who believe their lives are subject to the control of others have an external locus of control. Work should be aimed at assisting the family to regain more control over their lives, sometimes by explaining how certain problem behaviours can develop and what action can be taken to decrease them, while at the same time increasing pro-social ones, to the advantage (and relief) of the child in question and of the rest of the family.

The next example demonstrates how clear, simple advice, based on a knowledge of SLT, can help families with a common behavioural problem.

CASE EXAMPLE: **Josh**

Josh, aged six, lives with his parents and baby sister in a house on an army base. The parents have been told that their son is 'developmentally delayed'. He goes to the local school, a choice made by his parents. In common with many army families, the family has moved around the country a great deal, with the result that they find it difficult to build up social networks. Neither parent has relatives living near. Josh's mother is resourceful but, with two young children, she lives in comparative social isolation.

Josh is physically robust, restless, energetic, moving constantly from one activity to another. His mother finds him exhausting. He appears to cope fairly well at school, although his teachers find it difficult to hold his interest. He cannot yet read or write but has speech and can follow simple instructions.

Josh's mother asked her GP for help with his sleeping problems. He will not go to bed at night, comes down the stairs, wants to watch videos, asks for a drink and 'leaps around the room'. The family was visited by a community nurse, who listened, observed and made some suggestions about paying Josh attention when he is 'playing nicely', playing quiet games with him before bedtime or reading to him, then offering him a warm, milky drink before finally taking (not ordering) him up to bed. When his mother and father protested that 'it wouldn't work, he'll come down again', they were told to 'be firm'. These simple instructions, especially the nurse's last imperative (be firm!), had a great effect: the parents supported each other to maintain this new regime ('you have to back each other up'); and within a week, Josh's bedtime behaviour had greatly improved. He now only occasionally comes downstairs, obtains no attention when he does so, and soon goes back to bed.

Comment

There are, of course, other areas of this family's life where support could be given, as will be evident from the family context. However, the evidence is that a child's behaviour problems can escalate, exasperate parents and at times end in over-chastisement (Cigno, 1995b). By prioritising problems, using the ASPIRE process model, Josh's bedtime behaviour emerged as the first issue to concentrate on. Lack of 'time off' in child care, together with tiredness at the end of the day, can result for children and adults in fractiousness and frayed tempers, particularly when there are other dependent children (in this case, a baby) needing physical care. Parents, too, need some time for themselves, to be 'just man and wife', as this mother put it. Successful intervention producing favourable change in one comparatively small area of people's lives not only improves other aspects but, as in this case, may impart a way of coping which is transferable to other areas.

Sometimes a simple model helps an understanding of events and provides new strategies for therapeutic intervention. The key to advising any specific course of action is careful observation and assessment. When this is not done, then the strategy will most likely fail. Along with the inconsistency of mediators (be firm!), this is a major reason why planned cognitive–behavioural intervention fails. This point is illustrated by Burke (1998c) with the example of a psychologist who advised a mother to encourage her child to eat at the table by providing little presents wrapped in paper as a reinforcer for her compliance. Children usually like unwrapping objects, hence the long-lasting success of the party game 'pass the parcel' and other similar celebratory events, like opening presents at Christmas. However, the practitioner failed to take into account that the child was unable to unwrap the presents and therefore did not make the association between the reinforcer (the wrapped presents) and the desired behaviour (compliance with eating at the table). The technique would work with a child able to make such an association but the enterprise is doomed if the child lacks this level of ability.

The following case example describes a successful outcome for a child with eating problems, following advice from a psychologist. The plan worked because of the appropriateness of the task and the experience for the child of early success, accompanied by social reinforcement, instead of failure. The full context of the case is described in order to gain a deeper appreciation of family involvement and commitment to helping their daughter.

CASE EXAMPLE: **Susan**

Susan is a nine-year-old girl who lives with her parents in a modern, detached house in a small village location. She has an older sister of 11 and a younger brother of five. Her learning disability was not diagnosed at birth but infantile spasms and difficulties in learning to talk eventually led to the diagnosis of severe developmental delay.

Susan is ambulant but has a tendency to fall. She cannot dress herself. She and her parents can use Makaton sign language. At home, Susan's sister is protective of her but her younger brother is less tolerant because she likes to play with his toys, excluding him from her game-playing. Neither have a very well-developed sense of sharing, making them in some ways not dissimilar in levels of intellectual and motor development.

Susan attends a special school and uses the hostel facilities which the school offers to all day children. This, plus the occasional weekend when Susan stays with foster carers, provides much-needed respite care for the family. Such opportunities mean that the parents do not have to worry about their daughter's needs for short periods, during which the rest of the family have a 'sense of normality'. They particularly value the experience of less restricted opportunities to go shopping as well as taking part in social engagements with family and friends.

Relatives and neighbours are helpful and will look after all the children when needed, allowing the parents some time together. The mother and father consider this to be a necessary time when they can talk. At present, family concerns are for the future: they do not want Susan to leave home, but nor do they wish the burden of care to fall on her brother and sister in years to come.

Professional involvement has been considerable. Susan has regularly visited the paediatrician, who monitored the spasms, now ceased, following the provision of suitable medication. Physiotherapy helped in the early years and continues in order to monitor her needs. She has been provided with special splints and supportive boots. School staff have been very helpful with information. Susan loves attending school and staying in the hostel for an overnight stay, or at the weekends, when space is available.

The educational psychologist was, according to her mother, a little unrealistic concerning Susan's ability to understand a 'reward programme': 'He seemed too laid back, even I didn't understand half of what he said.' However, she did follow his advice regarding Susan's problems with eating too much too quickly and choking on her food. (It had already been established that there was no medical reason for this tendency to choke.) Susan was taught to eat correctly by the introduction of a simplified system of feeding. This was achieved by presenting food in small pieces, one at a time, and waiting until each piece was finished before introducing the next, accompanied by encouraging smiles and words from the parent. This simple, step-by-step approach also provided its own reward; because Susan's mouth never became too full, choking was avoided, and the meal enjoyed. Susan can now eat at a slower speed, not only at home but also at school and in other social situations.

Comment

Susan's immediate family is making the best of their situation. They have a wider circle of family and friends who are able to help, but also make use of various professional services. Needs within the family can be identified at individual, sibling, family and partnership level, although fulfilment of certain of these needs at times excludes Susan. This is not uncommon, as other of our examples show, particularly where meeting siblings' needs is concerned (see

Chapter 6). Providing extra time for Susan's brother and sister as well as for the parents themselves as a couple has helped establish a better balance of relationships within the whole family.

Despite her doubts, Susan's mother did implement the psychologist's programme to help her eating problems, with positive results. It is a good example of a clear, specific intervention, based on research evidence of 'what works', which has wider beneficial repercussions for other family members and in other situations, yet is little used in the social work field (see Cigno & Bourn (1998) for examples of a cognitive–behavioural approach in a wide variety of social work situations and settings; and Macdonald & Roberts (1995) for a study of what works in the early years).

Additionally, allowing Susan to experience breaks from home helps her parents to be less protective and anxious, and to learn to see their child as an individual with some independence of her own. It also promotes both the individuality of each family member and a sense of family cohesion when all the family is together again. Short-term breaks, according to the research by Booth (1990), are an essential service for maintaining family cohesion, while different types of informal support help to reduce the impact of stresses and strains. It is clear, therefore, that utilising informal and formal care together with specific interventions as required enables families to adapt and to cope with their situation, acts as a barrier to stress and engenders a sense of family life in the process.

Conclusion

Families meet numerous professionals who assess medical and social needs, monitor progress and offer services. They may provide advice on how to care, manage and cope with life-changing events on the one hand, and with specific problems in the family on the other, rendering coordination of service provision not only necessary but essential. Parents prefer a 'named person' – a keyworker – as we have shown in our 1995 research (Burke & Cigno, 1996); a coordinated approach has the advantage that families know who to turn to, are less confused by the variety and variability of contacts, and decision-making is better informed. The aim is for a seamless service to ensure that positive practice becomes a reality (see Chapter 10).

Working in partnership is central to child care work and means working with the child as well as the parents. The opportunity for oppression by omission or commission is minimised when no individual need is left out. It is evident, though, that families face problems and uncertainties with ambivalence, since they need a service, but are unsure that the service provided will both meet the identified need and be delivered in a sympathetic way. The sense of 'fighting for our child's rights' may become established as an entrenched response, if support and services are extracted rather than offered, or negotiated in partnership.

Overcoming this ambivalent stance, which is a protective cover against hurt and disappointment adopted by some parents, requires experiences of positive practice, where the gains are real, people are listened to and listening results in thorough, careful assessments, realistic promises and the provision of resources within clearly defined financial and legal restraints. Over-optimism on the part of professionals may initially be reassuring to families but in the longer term becomes a reason for their resentment. On the other hand, families feel stigmatised if they are made to feel grateful for the delivery of inadequate resources. Instead, we need to promote a form of practice that gives a sense of dignity, choice and entitlement to services. These are matters of citizens' rights. Professionals need to ground their practice in reality while at the same time, on a wider front, encourage advocacy for and from children and families whom they are employed to help.

Being a child with learning disabilities is not easy. Neither is being a carer, a brother or a sister of such a child. In a civilised society, it is not too much to ask that, first, the disadvantage and extra pressures involved do not lie where they fall but are recognised and shared; and second, other people and institutions change in order to provide an environment where the children and families in question are fully included.

Chapter 12

Postscript

In this book we have been concerned to promote an increased awareness and understanding, particularly for professionals, of children with learning disabilities. These final words are by way of a brief summing-up of the essence of the book's message.

First, a message for children, young people and their carers. We write from our long experience, in various forms, of being carers and individuals with disabilities. Our earlier book (Burke & Cigno, 1996) was a research monograph with a different appeal. The report on which it was based, though, was distributed to almost all parents who took part in the study and, to our delight, used by families in campaigns for services. We hope that this practical use of our work will be repeated, and that you will find some reflections of your own experiences in the illustrations and case examples.

Second, a message for the practitioner–researcher. We are also social workers; and one of us still spends part of the week as an employee in a social services department. We urge you to initiate your own enquiries into the area of personal and professional responsibility concerning disabilities generally, and in the area of children with learning disabilities in particular. Our desire is to promote interest and foster best practice, which can be achieved by a constant searching for what constitutes best practice. It is hard work, but worth it.

The very last words are left to a mother, as she reflects on the life of her severely disabled son, Matthew. The quote illustrates the importance of placing an unconditional value on the person and highlights the strengths and spirit of children with disabilities and their carers. Matthew, encountered earlier, was aged 13 years at the time of the interview with his mother:

'Matthew had not eaten food for four years, always depending on nasogastric feeding. But slowly the weaning off of tube feeding was accomplished and he swallowed, first custard, just two spoonsful, then months later, whole tins of baby food – only one spoonful at a time! Once, when giving him a taste of ice-cream he made a sound, like 'more'. When given a further helping he smiled, for the first time since his debilitating illness. Now, many years later, he still does not speak, but smiles with contentment when fed his favourite food. The sense of achievement is still as if he got a double first at Oxford, except in some ways Matthew's achievements, with his level of disadvantage, seem all the greater.'

References

Abbott, P. & Sapsford, R. (1988) *Community Care for Mentally Handicapped Children*. Open University Press, Milton Keynes.

Ackoff, R.L. (1985) *On Conceptions of Professions*. Social Systems Sciences Department, University of Philadelphia, Philadelphia.

Action for Children (1995) *All in the Family*. Action for Children, London.

Adams, R. (1996) *Social Work and Empowerment* (2nd edn). Macmillan, London.

Advocacy in Action (1993) Review of Williams, P. & Schultz, B. (1982, 1991) *We Can Speak for Ourselves: Self-Advocacy by Mentally Handicapped People*. Souvenir Press, Nottingham.

Allen, J. (1998) *Actively Seeking Inclusion: Pupils with Special Needs in Mainstream Schools*. Falmer, London.

Anon (1989) A parent's diary. In: *Making Connections: Reflecting on the Lives and Experiences of People with Learning Difficulties* (eds A. Brechin & J. Walmsley). Hodder & Stoughton/Oxford University Press, London.

Appleton, P.L., Boll, V., Everett, J.M., Kelly, A.M, Meredith, K.H. & Payne, T.G. (1997) Beyond child development centres: care coordination for children with disabilities. *Child Care, Health and Development*, **23**, 29–40.

Aspis, S. (1999) People with learning difficulties can speak for themselves [letter] *Community Care*, 24–30 June, 13.

Atkinson, D. (1989) *Someone to Turn to: the Social Worker's Role and the Role of Frontline Staff in Relation to People with Mental Handicaps*. British Institute for Mental Handicap Publications, Kidderminster.

Atkinson, D. & Williams, P. (1990) *Networks: Workbook 2*. Open University, Department of Health and Social Welfare, Milton Keynes.

Atkinson, N. & Crawforth, M. (1995) *All in the Family: Siblings and Disability*. NCH Action for Children, London.

Audit Commission (1994) *Seen but not Heard: Coordinating Community Child Health and Social Services for Children in Need*. HMSO, London.

Ayer, S. & Alaszewski, A. (1984) *Community Care and the Mentally Handicapped: Services for Mothers and their Mentally Handicapped Children*. Croom Helm, London.

Baker, B.L. & Brightman, A.J. (1997) *Steps to Independence: Second Report of an SSI Project on Transition Services for Disabled Young People*. Department of Health, HMSO, London.

Baker, B.L., Landen, S.J. & Kashima, K.J. (1991) Effects of parent training on families of children with mental retardation – increased burden or generalised benefit? *American Journal of Mental Retardation*, 96, 127–136.

Bakken, J., Miltenberger, R.G. & Schauss, S. (1993) Teaching parents with mental retardation. *American Journal on Mental Retardation*, 97, 404–417.

Baldwin, S. (1985) *The Costs of Caring: Families with Disabled Children*. Routledge & Kegan Paul, London.

Baldwin, S. & Carlisle, J. (1994) *Social Support for Disabled Children and their Families: a Review of the Literature*. Social Services Inspectorate, HMSO, Edinburgh.

Baldwin, S., Baser, D. & Harding, K. (1991) *Multi-Level Needs Assessment*. British Association of Behavioural Psychotherapy, London.

Ball, M. (1998) *Disabled Children: Directions for their Future Care*. Department of Health/Social Services Inspectorate, HMSO, London.

Barclay Report (1982) *Social Workers: their Role and Tasks*. National Institute for Social Work, London.

Barnes, M. (1997) *Care, Communities and Citizens*. Longman, Harlow.

Barr, N. (1999) Genetic counselling: a consideration of the potential and key obstacles to assisting parents adapt to a child with learning disabilities. *British Journal of Learning Disabilities*, 17, 30–36.

Beck, U. & Beck-Gersheim, E. (1995) *The Normal Chaos of Love*. Penguin, Harmondsworth.

Becker, S., Aldridge, J. & Dearden, C. (1998) *Young Carers and their Families*. Blackwell Science, Oxford.

Bender, M. & Valletutti, G. (1976) *Teaching the Moderately and Severely Handicapped*. University Park Press, Baltimore.

Beresford, B. (1994) *Positively Parents: Caring for a Severely Disabled Child*. HMSO, London.

Beresford, B. (1997) *Personal Accounts: Involving Disabled Children in Research*. Social Policy Research Unit, University of York, Stationery Office, London.

Bernal, M.E. (1984) Consumer issues in parent training. In: *Parent Training: Foundations of Research and Practice* (eds R.F. Dangel & R.A. Polster). Guilford Press, New York.

Bijou, S. (1976) *Child Development*. Prentice Hall, Englewood Cliffs.

Blackard, M.K. & Barsch, E.T. (1982) Parents' and professionals' perceptions of the handicapped child's impact on the family. *Journal of the Association of the Severely Handicapped*, 7, 62–70.

Boateng, P. (1998) On a promissory note ... *Community Care* (Inside), 30 July–5 August, 1.

Bond, H. (1999) Difficult transitions. *Community Care,* 29 July–4 August, 32.

Bone, M. & Meltzer, H. (1989) *The Prevalence of Disability Among Children.* Office of Population Censuses and Surveys, HMSO, London.

Booth, T. (1990) *Better Lives: Changing Services for People with Learning Difficulties.* Joint Unit for Social Services Research, University of Sheffield, Sheffield.

Booth, T. & Booth, W. (1993) Parenting for learning difficulties: lessons for practitioners. *British Journal of Social Work,* 23, 459–480.

Booth, T. & Booth, W. (1994) *Parenting Under Pressure: Mothers and Fathers with Learning Difficulties.* Open University Press, Buckingham.

Bulmer, M. (ed.) (1985) *Essays on the History of British Sociological Research.* Cambridge University Press, Cambridge.

Burghes, L. (1994) *Lone Parenthood and Family Disruption: the Outcomes for Children, Occasional Paper 18.* Family Policy Studies Centre, London.

Burke, P. (1991) Best of both worlds. *Social Work Today,* 13 June, 22, 39.

Burke, P. (1993) Oppressive practices and child disability. In: *The State, the Family and the Child* (eds G. Bradley & K. Wilson). University of Hull, Hull.

Burke, P. (1997a) *Children and Young People with Learning Disabilities: Facing Changes and Transitional Developments.* Paper presented to the Sixth European Congress, International Society for the Prevention of Child Abuse and Neglect, Barcelona.

Burke, P. (1997b) Children with learning disabilities: primary prevention social work with families. *Journal of Child Centred Practice,* 4, 93–100.

Burke, P. (1998a) *'Thoughts which live too deep for tears.' Working with Children with Learning Disabilties and their Families.* Paper presented to the International Society for the Prevention of Child Abuse and Neglect, Twelfth World Congress, Aukland.

Burke, P. (1998b) Elements of risk and supervision: evaluating outcome decisions. In: *The Working of Social Work,* (eds J. Cheetham & M. Kazi) Jessica Kingsley, London.

Burke, P. (1998c) Children with severe learning disabilities. In: *Cognitive–Behavioural Social Work Practice* (eds K. Cigno & D. Bourn). Ashgate, Aldershot.

Burke, P. (1999) Social service staff: risks they face and their dangerousness to others, In: *Risk Assessment in Social Care and Social Work* (ed. P. Parsloe), *Research Highlights in Social Work 36.* Jessica Kingsley, London.

Burke, P. (2000) 'Special needs children.' In *Blackwell Encyclopedia of Social Work* (ed. M. Davies), Blackwell Science, Oxford.

Burke, P. & Cigno, K. (1995) *Children with Learning Disabilities and the Need for Family Support Networks. Research report published for the Children's Research Fund.* University of Hull, Hull.

Burke, P. & Cigno, K. (1996) *Support for Families: Helping Children with Learning Disabilities.* Ashgate, Aldershot.

Burke, P. & Cigno. K. (1997) The need for family support networks. *International Journal of Child and Family Welfare,* **2,** 47–60.

Burke, P., Manthorpe, J. & Cigno, K. (1997) Relocating prevention in practice. *Journal of Learning Disabilities for Nursing, Health and Social Care,* **1,** 176–180.

Burke, P. & Montgomery, S. (2000) *Siblings of Children with Disabilities: Pilot Study.* Research report published for the Children's Research Fund, University of Hull, Hull.

Busfield, J. (1987) Parenting and parenthood. In: *Policy is Personal: Sex, Gender and Informal Care* (ed. G. Cohen). Tavistock, London.

Butler, N et al. (1978) *Handicapped Children: their Homes and Lifestyles.* Department of Child Health, University of Bristol, Bristol.

Byrne, E.A., Cunningham, C.C. & Sloper, P. (1988) *Families and their Children with Down's Syndrome: One Feature in Common.* Routledge, London.

Cairns, I. (1992) The health of mothers and fathers with a child with a disability. *Health Visitor,* **65,** 238–239.

CCETSW (1995) *Assuring Quality in Social Work: Rules and Requirements for the DipSW.* Central Council for Education and Training in Social Work, London.

Chambra, R., Ahmad, M., Hirst, M., Lawton, D. & Beresford, B. (1999) *Ethnic Minority Families Caring for a Severely Disabled Child.* Polity Press, London.

Chetwynd, J. (1985) Factors contributing to stress in mothers caring for an intellectually handicapped child. *British Journal of Social Work,* **15,** 295–304.

Cigno, K (1988) Consumer views of a family centre drop-in. *British Journal of Social Work,* **18,** 361–375.

Cigno, K. (1995a) The person not the disability. *Journal of Interprofessional Care,* **9,** 7–8.

Cigno, K. (1995b) Helping to prevent abuse: a behavioural approach with families. In: *The Child Protection Handbook* (eds K. Wilson & A. James). Bailliere Tindall, London.

Cigno, K. & Bourn, D. (eds) (1998) *Cognitive-Behavioural Social Work in Practice,* Ashgate, Aldershot.

Cigno, K. with Burke, P. (1997) Single mothers of children with learning disabilities: an undervalued group. *Journal of Interprofessional Care,* **11,** 177–186.

Cigno, K. & Gore, J. (1998) *An Evaluation of the Multi-agency Children's Centre.* University of Hull, Hull.

Cigno, K. & Gore, J. (1999) A seamless service: meeting the needs of children with disabilities through a multi-agency approach. *Child and Family Social Work,* **4,** 325–35.

Closs, A. (1998) Quality of life of children and young people with serious medical conditions. In: *Growing Up with Disability, Research Highlights in Social Work 34* (eds C. Robinson & K. Stalker). Jessica Kingsley, London.

Coleman, S.V. (1990) The sibling of the retarded child: self-concept, deficit compensation, motivation and perceived parental behaviour. *Dissertation Abstracts International,* 51 (10–13), 5023.

Cooke, K. & Lawton, D. (1984) Informal support for the carers of disabled children. *Child Care, Health and Development,* 10, 67–69.

Corby, B. (1993) *Child Abuse: Towards a Knowledge Base.* Open University Press, Buckingham.

Craft, A. & Brown, H. (1994) Personal relationships and sexuality: the staff role. In: *Practice Issues in Sexuality and Learning Disabilities* (ed. A. Craft). Routledge, London.

Cross, S.B., Kaye, E. & Ratnofsky, A.C. (1993) *A Report on the Maltreatment of Children With Disabilities.* National Centre for Child Abuse and Neglect, Washington, DC.

Dale, N. (1996) *Working with Families with Special Needs: Partnership and Practice.* Routledge, London.

Dalrymple, J. & Burke, B. (1995) *Anti-oppressive Practice: Social Care and the Law.* Open University Press, Buckingham.

Daly, N. (1998) Cause for optimism. *Community Care,* 29 October–4 November, 9.

Dawson, C. & Morgan, P. (1998) *Learning Disabilities and Mental Illness: a Guide for Practitioners and Carers.* Pepar Publications, Birmingham.

Dean, M. (1994) *Critical and Effective Histories.* Routledge, London.

De'Ath, E. (1985) *Self-help and Family Centres: a Current Initiative in Helping the Community.* National Children's Bureau, London.

Department of Education (1994) *Code of Practice on the Identification and Assessment of Special Needs.* HMSO, London.

Department of Health (1989) *Caring for People: Community Care in the Next Decade and Beyond.* HMSO, London.

Department of Health (1991) *The Children Act 1989: Guidance and Regulations. Volume 6. Children with Disabilities: a New Framework for the Care and Upbringing of Children.* HMSO, London.

Department of Health (1995) *Child Protection: Messages from Research.* HMSO, London.

Department of Health (1998) *Modernising Health and Social Services: National Priorities Guidance.* Stationery Office, London.

Department of Health (1999) *Caring about Carers: a National Strategy for Carers.* HMSO, London.

Department of Health (2000) *Lost in Care: Report of the Tribunal of Inquiry into the Abuse of Children in Care in the Former County Council Areas of Gwynedd and Clwyd since 1974.* The Stationery Office, London.

Department of Health and Social Security (1971) *Better Services for the Mentally Handicapped.* Cm 4683. HMSO, London.

Department of Health and Social Security (1972) *Report of the Committee on Nursing.* Cm 5115. HMSO, London.

Department of Health and Social Security (1980) *Development Team for the Mentally Handicapped, second report 1978–79.* HMSO, London.

Department of Health and Social Welfare (1986) *Mental Handicap: Patterns for Living.* Paper 555. Open University Press, Buckingham.

Department of Health, Home Office, Department for Education and Employment (1999) *Working Together to Safeguard Children: New Government Guidance on Inter-agency Cooperation.* Stationery Office, London.

Dobson, B. & Middleton, S. (1998) *Paying to Care: the Cost of Childhood Disability.* Joseph Rowntree Foundation, York.

Dominelli, L. (1997) *Anti-Racist Social Work,* 2nd edn. Practice Social Work Series. British Association of Social Workers/Macmillan Press, London.

Donohue-Colletta, N. (1992) *Cross-cultural Child Development: a Training Course for Program Staff.* Christian Children's Fund, Richmond, VA.

Donovan, P. (1999) Home Office pushes for mandatory video evidence from children in sexual abuse cases. *Community Care,* 24–30 June, 32.

Dyer, C. (1999) Bar on vasectomy for disabled son. *Guardian,* 1 August, 5.

Dyson, L.L. (1996) The experience of families of children with learning disabilities: parental stress, family functioning and sibling self-concept. *Journal of Learning Disabilities,* 29, 280–286.

Editorial (1993) Young carers overlooked. *Care Weekly,* October 28, 3.

Eigher, W. (1998) Working towards human rights and social justice. [Editorial] *Inclusion,* 20, 1.

Ellis, R. & Hendry, E.B. (1998) Do we all know the score? *Child Abuse Review,* 7, 360–363.

Etzioni, A. (1969) *The Semi-professions and their Organization: Teachers, Nurses, Social Workers.* Free Press, New York.

Evandrou, M. (1990) *Challenging the invisibility of carers: mapping informal care nationally.* Discussion Paper WSP/49. September. London School of Economics, London.

Farmer, E. (1997) Protection and child welfare: striking the balance. In: *Child Protection and Family Support: Tensions, Contradictions and Possibilities* (ed. N. Parton). Routledge, London.

Finer Report (1974) *Report of the Committee on One-Parent Families,* 2 vols, Cm 5629. Department of Health and Social Security, HMSO, London.

Finklestein, V. (1993) *Workbook 1: Being Disabled.* Open University Press, Milton Keynes.

Fitton, P. (1994) *Listen to Me: Communicating the Needs of People with Profound Intellectual and Multiple Disabilities.* Jessica Kingsley, London.

Fivush, R., Gray, J.T. & Fromhoff, F.A. (1987) Two-year-olds talk about the past. *Cognitive Development,* **2,** 393–409.

Fletcher, K. (1999) Essence of Best Value. *Community Care,* 24–30 June, 32.

Friel, J. (1995) *Children with Special Needs: Assessment, Law and Practice – Caught in the Acts,* 3rd edn. Jessica Kingsley, London.

Frude, N. (1991) *Understanding Family Problems: a Psychological Approach.* Wiley & Sons, Chichester.

Gambrill, E. (1983) *Casework: a Competency-based Approach.* Prentice-Hall, Englewood Cliffs.

Gardner, A. & Smyly, S.R. (1997) How do we stop 'doing' and start listening: responding to the emotional needs of people with learning disabilities. *British Journal of Learning Disabilities,* **25,** 26–29.

Gath, A. (1974) Sibling reactions to mental handicap: a comparison of the brothers and sisters of mongol children. *Journal of Child Psychology and Psychiatry,* **15,** 187–198.

Gault, M. (1999) We are not prisoners of our past. *Community Care,* 15–21 July, 17.

Glendinning, C. (1986) *A Single Door: Social Work with the Families of Disabled Children.* Allen & Unwin, London.

Goodinge, S. (1998) *Removing Barriers for Disabled Children: Inspection of Services to Disabled Children and their Families.* Department of Health/Social Services Inspectorate, London.

Gorell Barnes, G., Thompson, P., Daniel, G. & Burchardt, N. (1998) *Growing Up in Stepfamilies.* Clarendon Press, Oxford.

Grant, G. (1992) Researching user and carer involvement in mental handicap services. In: *Researching User Involvement* (eds M. Barnes & G. Wistow). Institute for Health Studies, University of Leeds, Leeds.

Green, H. (1985) *Informal Carers.* General Household Survey, OPCS Supplement. HMSO, London.

Green, H. (1988) *Informal Carers.* General Household Survey, OPCS Supplement. HMSO, London.

Griffiths, R. (1988) *Community Care: Agenda for Action.* HMSO, London.

Grossman, H.J. (ed.) (1983) *Classification in Mental Retardation.* American Association on Mental Deficiency, Washington, DC.

Hall, D. (1997) Child development teams: are they fulfilling their purpose? *Child Care, Health and Development,* **23,** 87–99.

Hardiker, P. (1996) The legal and social construction of significant harm. In: *Child Welfare Services: Developments in Law, Policy, Practice and Research* (eds M. Hill & J. Aldgate). Jessica Kingsley, London.

Hardiker, P., Exton, K. & Barker, M. (1991) *Policies and Prevention in Child Care.* Gower, Aldershot.

Haskell, S.H. & Barrett, E.K. (1993) *The Education of Children with Physical and Neurological Disabilities,* 3rd edn. Chapman & Hall, London.

Henwood, M. (1998) Helping the helpers. *Community Care,* 13–19 August, 22.

Hill, M. (1998) What children and young people say they want from social services. *Research, Policy and Planning* 15, 17–27.

Hill, R. (1958) Generic features of families under stress. *Social Casework,* 49, 139–150.

Hopson, B. (1981) Transition, understanding and managing personal change. In: *Psychology for Social Workers* (ed. M. Herbert). Macmillan, London.

Hornby, G. (1992) A review of fathers' accounts of their experiences of parenting children with disabilities. *Disability, Handicap and Society,* 7, (4), 363–374.

Hubert, J. (1991) *Homebound: Crisis in the Care of Young People with Severe Learning Difficulties: a Story of 20 Families.* King's Fund Centre, London.

Hudson, B. (1995) Is a coordinated service attainable? In: *Services for People with Learning Disabilities* (ed. N. Malin). Routledge, London.

Hugman, R. (1991) *Power in the Caring Professions.* Macmillan, London.

Iwaniec, D. (1995) *The Emotionally Abused and Neglected Child.* Wiley, Chichester.

Jackson, E. & Jackson, N. (1999) *Helping People with a Learning Disability Explore Choice.* Jessica Kingsley, London.

James, A.L. & Wilson, K. (1986) *Couples, Conflict and Change: Social Work with Marital Relationships.* Tavistock, London.

Jenkinson, J.C. (1998) Parent choice in the education of students with disabilities. *International Journal of Disability, Development and Education,* 45, 189–202.

Jones, C. (1998) Early intervention: the eternal triangle. In: *Growing Up with Disability* (eds C. Robinson & K. Stalker). Jessica Kingsley, London.

Jones, E. & Ware, J. (1997) Early intervention services to children with special needs: a Welsh study. In: *Families in Context: Emerging Trends in Family Support and Early Intervention* (ed. B. Carpenter). David Fulton, London.

Jones, S. & Joss, R. (1995) Models of professionalism. In: *Learning and Teaching in Social Work: Towards Reflective Practice* (eds M. Yelloly & M. Henkel). Jessica Kingsley, London.

Kennedy, M. (1992) Not the only way to communicate: a challenge to voice in child protection work *Child Abuse Review,* 1, 169–77.

Kennedy, M. (1995) Perceptions of abused disabled children. In: *The Child Protection Handbook* (eds K. Wilson & A. James). Bailliere Tindall, London.

Kew, S. (1975) *Handicap and Family Crisis: a Study of the Siblings of Handicapped Children.* Pitman Publishing, London.

Kidd, R. & Hornby, G. (1993) Transfer from special to mainstream. *British Journal of Special Education,* 20, 17–19.

Kübler-Ross, E. (1969) *On Death and Dying.* Tavistock, London.

Kushlick, A., Dagnan, D. & Trower, P. (1998) Working with carers using the birthday exercise. In: *Cognitive–behavioural Social Work in Practice* (eds K. Cigno & D. Bourn). Ashgate, Aldershot.

La Fontaine, J. (1991) *Bullying: the Child's View. An Analysis of Telephone Calls to Childline about Bullying.* Calouste Gulbenkian Foundation, London.

Law Commission (1995) *Mental Incapacity.* Law Com. No 231. HMSO, London.

Lawton, M. (1993) From Startrack to Leisure Choice: the first slow steps toward change. In: *Disabling Barriers. Enabling Environments* (eds J. Swain, V. Finklestein, S. French & M. Oliver). Sage/Open University Press, London.

Lee, D., McGee, D. & Unger, S. (1998) Issues in the development of a computer-based safety programme for children with severe learning difficulties. *Child Abuse Review,* 7, 343–354.

Lefcourt, H.M. (1976) *Locus of Control: Current Trends in Theory and Research.* Lawrence Erlbaum, Hillsdale.

Lloyd, J.M. (1986) *Jacob's Ladder: a Parent's View of Portage.* Costello, Tunbridge Wells.

Lobato, D. (1983) Siblings of handicapped children: a review. *Journal of Autism and Developmental Disorders,* 13, 347–364.

Lobato, D. (1990) *Brothers, Sisters and Special Needs: Information and Activities for Helping Young Siblings of Children with Chronic Illnesses and Developmental Disabilities.* Paul H. Brookes, Baltimore, MD.

Lobato, D., Dunlap, D. & Hollingsworth, J. (1987) Psychosocial characteristics of pre-school siblings of handicapped and non-handicapped children, *Journal of Abnormal Child Psychology,* 5, 329–338.

Lockyer, T. & Gilbert, T. (1995) Levels of intervention. In: *Learning Disabilities: Practice Issues in Health Settings* (eds M. Todd & T. Gilbert). Routledge, London.

McCarthy, M. (1998) *Sexuality and Women with Learning Disabilities.* Jessica Kingsley, London.

McCormack, M.A. (1978) *A Mentally Handicapped Child in the Family.* Constable, London.

McCormack, M. (1992) *Special Children: Special Needs.* Thorsons, London.

Macdonald, G. & Roberts, H. (1995) *What Works in the Early Years?* Barnardos, London.

McGrath, M. (1991) *Multi-disciplinary Teamwork: Community Mental Handicap Teams.* Gower, Aldershot.

McGurk, H. & Glachan, M. (1988) Children's conversations with adults. *Children and Society,* 2, 20–34.

McHale, S.M. & Gamble, W.C. (1987) The role of siblings and peers. In: *Special Children, Special Risks: The Maltreatment of Children with*

Disabilities (eds J. Garbarino, P.E. Brookhauser & K.J. Authier). Aldine de Gruyter, New York.

McIntosh, A. (1992) *Caring at home for children and young adults with a mental handicap: the impact of service development in North Humberside.* Unpublished MPhil thesis, University of Hull

McIntosh, B. & Whittaker, A. (1998) *Days of Change.* King's Fund, London.

Maclean, M. & Eekelaar, J. (1997) *The Parental Obligation: a Study of Parenthood Across Households.* Hart Publishing, Oxford.

Manthorpe, J. (1994) The family and informal care. In: *Implementing Community Care* (ed. N. Malin). Open University Press, Buckingham.

Manthorpe, J. (1995) Services to families. In *Services for People with Learning Disabilities* (ed. N. Malin). Routledge, London.

May, D. & Hughes, D. (1985) The prospects of leaving school for the mildly mentally handicapped. *British Journal of Special Education,* **12** (4), 151–158.

Mayer, D.J. & Vadasy, P.F. (1997) *Sibshops: Workshops for Siblings of Children with Special Needs,* 2nd edn. Paul H. Brookes, Baltimore, MD.

Mencap (1999) *Living in Fear.* Campaigns Department, Mencap National Centre, London.

Middleton, L. (1998) Services for disabled children: integrating the perspective of the social workers. *Child and Family Social Work,* 3, 239–246.

Middleton, L. (1999) *Disabled Children: Challenging Social Exclusion.* Blackwell Science, Oxford.

Miles, R. (1994) *The Children We Deserve.* Harper Collins, London.

Moeller, C.T. (1986) The effect of professionals on the family of a handicapped child. In: *Families of Handicapped Children: Needs and Supports Across the Life Span* (eds R.R. Fewell & P.F. Vadasy). Pro-ed Inc., Texas.

Morris, J. (1995) *Gone Missing? A Research and Policy Review of Disabled Children Living Away from their Families.* Who Cares? Trust, London.

Morris, J. (1999) Disabled children, child protection systems and the Children Act 1989. *Child Abuse Review,* 8, 91–108.

Morrow, V. (1992) Terry Cunningham: a brother who sticks up for his siblings. *Parents and Friends Together for People with Deaf-blindness News,* 1, 2.

Mulhall, D. (1989) *Functional Performance Record.* NFER-Nelson, Windsor.

Murray, G. & Jampolsky, G.G. (eds) (1982) *Straight from the Siblings: Another Look at the Rainbow.* Celestial Arts, Berkeley, CA.

National Children's Home (1994) *Unequal Opportunities: Children with Disabilities and their Families Speak Out.* NCH Action for Children, London.

Oliver, M. (1990) *The Politics of Disablement.* Macmillan, Basingstoke.

Oliver, M. (1998) *Understanding Disability: from Theory to Practice.* Macmillan, London.

Oliver, M. & Barnes, C. (1998) *Disabled People and Social Policy* Social Policy in Britain Series. Longman, London.

Packman, J. (1981) *The Child's Generation*, 2nd Edn. Basil Blackwell & Martin Robertson, Oxford.

Pereira, C. (1989) Mothers and daughters. *African Women*, 4, 21.

Petr, C. & Barney, D.D. (1993) Reasonable efforts for children with disabilities: the parents' perspective. *Social Work*, 38, 247–255.

Pitkeathley, J. (1995) Pushed to the limits. *Community Care*, 25–31 May, 2.

Pollack, G. & Stewart, J. (1997) *The Disabled Child, the Family and the Professional.* Whiting & Birch, London.

Porter, G. & Kelly, B. (1998) The special educator and inclusion: a new reality. *Getting There: International Update on Inclusive Education*, 6, 4–6.

Powell, T.H. & Ogle, P.A. (1985) *Brothers and Sisters – a Special Part of Exceptional Families.* Paul & Brookes Publishing, Baltimore.

Randall, P.E. & Parker, J. (1999) *Helping Families with Autism.* John Wiley, Chichester.

Reason, L. (1994) *Partnerships in Practice: Professionals, Parents and Children Working Together.* Unpublished MSc dissertation, University of Hull.

Richardson, M. (1997) Reflections and celebrations – Neal (1960–1987): narrative of a young man with profound and multiple disabilities. *Journal of Learning Disabilities for Nursing, Health and Social Care*, 1 (4), 191–195.

Riddell, S. (1998) The dynamic of transition to adulthood. In: *Growing Up with Disability. Research Highlights in Social Work 34* (eds C. Robinson & K. Stalker). Jessica Kingsley, London.

Roberts, J. (1988) Why are some families more vulnerable to child abuse? In: *Early Prediction and Prevention of Child Abuse.* (eds K. Browne, L. Davies & P. Stratton) John Wiley, Chichester.

Roberts, K. & Lawton, D. (1999) *Reaching its Target? Disability Allowance for Children.* Social Policy Research Unit, University of York, York.

Roberts, H. & Wellard, S. (1997) Hear my voice. *Community Care*, 16 January, 24–25.

Ross, E. (1990) Unifying services for children with mental handicaps. In: *Combating Mental Handicap: a Multidisciplinary Approach* (eds P.L.C. Evans & A.D.B. Clarke). AB Academic Publishers, Oxford.

Rowe, A. & Goodman, L. (1995) Caring for the carers. *Community Care*, 27 April–3 May, 24.

Russell, P. (1994) Children with disabilities and special needs: current issues regarding child protection. In: *Refocus on Child Abuse: Medical, Legal and Social Work Perspectives* (ed. A. Levy). Hawksmere, Abingdon.

Sands, D.J. & Wehmeyer, M.L. (eds) (1996) *Self-determination Across the Lifespan*. Paul H. Brookes, London.

Schaffer, H.R. (1971) *The Growth of Stability*. Penguin, Harmondsworth.

Schreiber, M. (1984) Normal siblings of retarded persons. *Social Casework: the Journal of Contemporary Social Work, 65*, 420–427.

Seligman, M. (ed.) (1991) *The Family with a Handicapped Child*, 2nd edn. Allyn & Bacon, London.

Seligman, M. & Darling, R.B. (1989) *Ordinary Families, Special Children*. Guilford Press, New York.

Seligman, M.E.P. (1975) *Helplessness*. Freeman, San Francisco.

Sheerin, F. (1998) Parents with learning disabilities: a review of the literature. *Journal of Advanced Nursing, 28*, 126–133.

Sheldon, B. (1995) *Cognitive–behavioural Therapy: Research, Practice and Philosophy*. Routledge, London.

Silva, E. & Smart, C. (eds) (1998) *The New Family?* Sage, London.

Simeonnson, R.J. & Bailey, D.B. (1986) Family dimensions in early intervention. In: *Handbook of Early Childhood Intervention* (eds S.J. Meisels & J.P. Shonkoff). Cambridge University Press, Cambridge.

Simonoff, E., Bolton, P. & Rutter, M. (1996) Mental retardation: genetic findings, clinical implications and research agenda. *Journal of Child Psychology and Psychiatry, 37*, 259–280.

Sinclair, R. (1996) Children's and young people's participation in decision-making: the legal framework in social services and education. In: *Child Welfare Services: Developments in Law, Policy, Practice and Research* (eds M. Hill & J. Aldgate). Jessica Kingsley, London.

Singer, G.H.S. (1996) Continuing supports: helping families of children with acquired brain injury. In: *Children with Acquired Brain Injury* (eds G.H.S. Singer, A. Glang & J.M. Williams). Paul H. Brookes, Baltimore.

Sloper, P. & Turner, S. (1991) Factors related to stress and satisfaction with life in families of children with Down's syndrome. *Journal of Child Psychology and Psychiatry, 32*, 655–676.

Sloper, P. & Turner, S. (1992) Service needs of families of children with severe physical disabilities. *Child Care, Health and Development, 18*, 259–282.

Smart, C. & Neale, B. (1999) *Family Fragments?* Polity Press/Blackwell, Oxford.

Smith, H. & Brown, H. (1989) Whose community, whose care? In: *Making Connections: Reflecting on the Lives and Experiences of People with Learning Difficulties* (eds A. Brechin & J. Walmsley). Hodder & Stoughton/ Open University Press, London.

Smyth, M. & Robus, N. (1989) *The Financial Circumstances of Families with Disabled Children Living in Private Households*. Report 5, OPCS, Social Survey Division. HMSO, London.

Snaith, R. (ed.) (1989) *Neighbourhood Care and Social Policy.* HMSO, London.

Social Services Inspectorate (1997a) *Responding to Families in Need: Inspection of Assessment, Planning and Decision-making in Family Support Services.* Department of Health/HMSO, London.

Social Services Inspectorate (1997b) *Moving on Towards Independence: Second Report of an SSI Project on Transition Services for Disabled Young People.* Department of Health/HMSO, London.

Social Services Inspectorate (1998a) *Partners in Planning: Approaches to Planning Services for Children and their Families.* Department of Health/HMSO, London.

Social Services Inspectorate (1998b) *Disabled Children: Directions for their Future Care.* Department of Health/HMSO, London.

Social Services Inspectorate (1998c) *Removing Barriers for Disabled Children: Inspection of Services to Disabled Children and their Families.* Department of Health/HMSO, London.

Sourkes, B. (1990) Siblings count too. Candlelighters *Childhood Cancer Foundation Youth Newsletter,* **12**, 6.

Stalker, K. (1999) Some ethical and methodological issues in research with people with learning disabilities. *Disability and Society,* **13**, 5–19.

Stevenson, O. (1998) *Neglected Children: Issues and Dilemmas.* Blackwell Science, Oxford.

Sutton, C. (1994) *Social Work, Community Work and Psychology.* British Psychological Society, Leicester.

Sutton, C. & Herbert, M. (1992) *Mental Health: a Client Support Resource Pack.* NFER-Nelson, London.

Sutton, C. (1999) *Helping Families with Troubled Children: a Preventive Approach.* John Wiley & Son, Chichester.

Swain, J., Finkelstein, V., French, S. & Oliver, N. (eds) (1993) *Disabling Barriers Enabling Environments.* Sage/Open University Press, London.

Swift, C. & Levin, G. (1987) Empowerment: an emerging mental health technology. *Journal of Primary Prevention,* **8**, 71–95.

Tasker, F.L. & Golombok, S. (1997) *Growing Up in a Lesbian Family: Effects on Child Development.* Guilford Press, New York.

Thompson, A. (1995) Paradise Lost. *Community Care,* 25–31 May, 5.

Towell, D. (1997) Promoting a better life for people with learning disabilities and their families: a practical agenda for the new government. *British Journal of Learning Disabilities,* **25**, 90–94.

Twigg, J. & Atkin, K. (1995) Carers and services: factors mediating service provision. *Journal of Social Policy,* **1**, 5–30.

Tymchuk, A.J. & Feldman, M.A. (1991) Parents with mental retardation and their children: review of research relevant to professional practice. *Canadian Psychology,* **32**, 486–494.

United Nations (1989) *The Convention on the Rights of the Child.* United Nations Children Fund, Geneva.

Utting, D. (1995) *Family and Parenthood: Supporting Families, Preventing Breakdown.* Joseph Rowntree Foundation, York.

Utting, W. (1997) *People Like Us: the Report of the Review of the Safeguards for Children Living Away from Home.* Department Of Health/ Welsh Office/Stationery Office, London.

Valios, N. (1999) Who makes the decisions? *Community Care (In Focus),* 29 July–4 August, 12.

Ward, L. (ed.) (1998) *Innovations in Advocacy and Empowerment for People with Intellectual Disabilities.* Lisieux Hall, London.

Ward, L. & Simons, K. (1998) Practising partnership: involving people with learning difficulties in research. *British Journal of Learning Disabilities,* **26**, 128-131.

Warnock, N. (1998) *An Intelligent Person's Guide to Ethics.* Duckworth, London.

Warnock Report (1978) *Special Educational Needs: Report of the Committee of Enquiry into the Education of Handicapped Children and Young People.* HMSO, London.

Watson, J. (1991) The Queen. *Down Syndrome News,* **15**, 108.

Welch, M. (1998) Whose needs are we meeting? *Professional Social Work,* September, 6.

Wertheimer, A. (1998) *Changing Days.* King's Fund, London.

Westcott, H. (1998) Disabled children and disability. In: *Growing Up with Disability. Research Highlights in Social Work 34* (eds C. Robinson & K. Stalker). Jessica Kingsley, London.

Westcott, H. & Cross, M. (1996) *This Far and No Further: Towards Ending the Abuse of Disabled Children.* British Association of Social Work/Venture Press, Birmingham.

Weston, K. (1991) *Families we Choose: Lesbian, Gays and Kinship.* Columbia University Press, New York.

White, M. (1998) Boateng launches radical plan to smash Berlin Wall. *Community Care,* 17–23 September, i–1.

White, M. & Cameron, J. (1987) *Portage Early Education Programme* (Anglicised Version). NFER-Nelson, London.

Whitman, B.Y. & Accardo, P.J. (1993) The parent with mental retardation: a guide for human service practitioners. *Journal of Social Work and Human Sexuality,* 8, 123–136.

Williams, F. (1996) Race, welfare and community care: an historical perspective. In: *'Race' and Community Care* (eds W. Ahmad & K. Atkin). Open University Press, Buckingham.

Wilmott, P. & Mayne, S. (1983) *Families at the Centre. Occasional Papers on Social Administration No. 72.* Bedford Square Press/National Council for Voluntary Organisations, London.

Wistow, G. (1994) Community care futures. In: *Caring for People in the Community – the New Welfare* (ed. M. Titterton). Jessica Kingsley, London.

Wolfensberger, W. (1972) *The Principle of Normalisation in Human Services*. National Institute on Mental Retardation, Toronto.

WHO (1992) *The ICD-10 Classification of Mental and Behavioural Disorders: Clinical Descriptions and Diagnostic Guidelines*. World Health Organisation, Geneva.

Write Off (1998) Disability is excluded from Exclusion Unit [letter from Laura Middleton]. *Professional Social Work*, April, 5.

Yerbury, M. (1997) Issues in multidisciplinary teamwork for children with disabilities. *Child Care, Health and Development*, 23, 77–86.

Young Adults Transition Project (1998) *Profile of Disabled School Leavers in Lewisham and Southwark*. Working Paper 1, August. YATP/Optimum Health Services, NHS Trust, London.

Young Adults Transition Project (1999) *Transition: Views and Experiences of Young People and Carers*. Working Paper 3. YATP/Optimum Health Services, NHS Trust, London.

Young, M. & Willmott, P. (1957) *Family and Kinship in East London*. Routledge & Kegan Paul, London.

Yule, B. & Carr, J. (1987) *Behaviour Modification for People with Mental Handicaps*, 2nd edn. Croom Helm, New York.

Zatlow, G. (1992) Just a sister. *Momentum*, Autumn, 13–16.

Bibliography

Aldgate, J. & Tunstill, J. (1996) *Setting up Services for Children in Need,* HMSO, London.

Bornat, J., Pereira, C., Pilgrim, D. & Williams, F. (1993) *Community Care: a Reader.* Macmillan, Basingstoke.

Brechin, A. & Walmsley, J. (eds) (1989) *Making Connections: Reflecting on the Lives and Experiences of People with Learning Difficulties.* Hodder and Stoughton/Open University Press, London.

Cigno, K. (1997) Downsizing, restructuring, purchasing and providing: social work and social services in a value-for-money climate. *International Journal of Sociology and Social Policy,* 17, 87–96.

Cigno, K. & Bourn, D. (eds) (1998) *Cognitive–Behavioural Social Work in Practice.* Ashgate, Aldershot.

Cohen, G. (1987) *Policy is Personal: Sex, Gender and Informal Care.* Tavistock, London.

Ferri, E. & Smith, K. (1998) *Step-parenting in the 1990s,* Family Policy Studies Centre, London.

Hill, M. & Aldgate, J. (1996) The Children Act 1989 and recent developments in research in England and Wales. In: *Child Welfare Services: Developments in Law, Policy, Practice and Research* (eds M. Hill & J. Aldgate). Jessica Kingsley, London.

Malin, N. (1995) *Services for People with Learning Disabilities.* Routledge, London.

Oliver, M. (1991) *Social Work, Disabled People and Disabling Environments,* Research Highlights in Social Work 21. Jessica Kingsley, London.

Parker, K.G. (1990) *With Due Care and Attention.* Family Policy Studies Centre, London.

Robinson, C. & Stalker, K. (eds) (1998) *Growing Up with Disability. Research Highlights in Social Work 34.* Jessica Kingsley, London.

Roll, J. (1991) *What is a Family?* Family Policy Studies Unit, London.

Seligman, M. & Darling, R.B. (1991) Ordinary families, special children: a systems approach to childhood disability. In: *The Family with a Handicapped Child,* 2nd edn (ed. M. Seligman). Allyn & Bacon, London.

Sylva, K. (1996) *Evaluation of the High/Scope Programme.* Oxford University Press, Oxford.

Index